Getting There & Staying There

Coaching Questions to Get There and Stay

_____

PRISCILLA H. DOUGLAS

Library of Congress Control Number: 2013913220

Printed in the U.S.A

16 15 14 13 1 2 3 4 5

ISBN-13: 978-0-9896484-0-0
ISBN-10: 0989648400

Sources:
The interested reader who wishes to pursue items cited will find references
in the text, with these exceptions:
The story of "Richard Parkes" on page 61 is from the Telegraph, April 16,
2010, and can be found at http://www.telegraph.co.uk/relationships/7594124/
Having-an-affair-One-mans-fall-from-grace.html

The story of Rene-Thierry Magon on pages 62 and 63 is from the
Daily News, December 27, 2008 why.http://articles.nydailynews.com/
2008-12- 27/news/17912606_1_scheme-house-arrest-luxury and from:
http://www.findingdulcinea.com/news/business/2008/December/
CEO-Dead-in-Presumed-Madoff-Related-Suicide.html

Cover design by KHJ Brand Integration
Interior design by Anne Rolland

"*Getting There and Staying There* is a candid, practical and wise blueprint to navigating a successful career and becoming an effective leader. Priscilla's book presents sharp and prescriptive insights that will benefit business leaders, political leaders and entrepreneurs.

—*Jerry L. Johnson*
Managing Director, RLJ Equity Partners

"This is a wise, provocative, and uplifting book that is loaded with artful descriptions of real-world situations based on Priscilla's years of experience coaching executives. The book challenges us to take control of our future—in our careers and in our lives—in pragmatic and thoughtful ways. By posing specific questions, Priscilla leads us to be proactive; and *do* something. In the end, we come to understand that where there is change, there is also opportunity to get where we want to go and to stay there."

—*Mike Jeans*
President, New Directions, Inc.

"*Getting There and Staying There* brilliantly guides the reader in how to manage and navigate one's career. Real-life examples coupled with thoughtful questions create a practical framework that can be applied effectively by both early-stage professionals and seasoned executives. Priscilla Douglas, a highly regarded and desired executive coach, provides sound advice that should help catapult anyone's career."

—*Bennie Wiley*
Former President and CEO, The Partnership, Inc.

"Priscilla Douglas has written an outstanding book that will make all of us think about what it means to be a leader. The book is a wonderful example of the ways those with no experience or with lots of experience can approach being leaders in business."

—*Charles J. Ogletree, Jr.*
Jesse Climenko Professor of Law, Founder and Executive Director,
The Charles Hamilton Houston Institute for Race and Justice

To my mentor, who believed in me:
Mel Howards

To my boss who encouraged me to soar:
Melvin H. "Mel" King

By his example, I learned the power of questions:
to Judge William H. Webster

Getting There &
Staying There

Acknowledgments

Sometimes I have to pinch myself because my friends are so generous and responsive. I have always surrounded myself with people who lift me higher and it has been so affirming that that is exactly what has happened during the process of writing this book. I have realized a goal that had been out of reach until now and *Zowie!* do I feel a sense of accomplishment! Some days it has felt like "Mr. Toad's wild ride" but thank goodness my friends' perfectly timed words and encouragement have kept me from bouncing off task.

My friends and family jumped for joy when I told then that I had moved from writing articles to really writing a book. So it is no surprise that many examples in this book include "my friend" so-and-so (some friends said it was OK to use their names while others preferred not). My heartfelt thanks for words of wisdom from Barbara Alleyne, Maddy Bragar, Sharon Buzard, Elizabeth Cook, Katye Hanley, Yvonne Jackson, Kathleen Knight, Douglas Marshall, MaryJo Meisner, Natalie McKenzie, Colette Phillips, Maia Porche, Rollins Ross, Beatrice St. Laurent, Shelley Stewart, Phil Tortorella, Susie White and my White House Fellows friends Carolyn Chin, Tom Shull, Chips Stewart, Jim Padilla and Mike Ullman.

I couldn't paint an accurate picture of the getting-there experience without the input of thirty-plus year olds Evelyn Barahona, Stephanie Fritz, Ben Olds and Jay Tuli, who shared what they have learned navigating their careers. They are not only accomplished, they are engaged and already giving back. I sincerely appreciate your insight and your generosity.

Many thanks to my hawk-eyed proofreaders, Edith Sandra Lambert and Susie White, and to administrative assistant Mary Foley who always keeps my path clear. And this book would still be a dream if not for the talent and insightful partnership that I developed with Perry McIntosh. Perry heard me speak at an event and she not only understood my voice, she helped me to find my voice by writing. She always provides an imaginative phrase or a way to streamline my words without being heavy handed. In fact Perry brings flow to *Getting There and Staying There*. Thanks to Perry, I am eager to begin work on my next book.

I especially want to thank my many clients and client companies; I have had the privilege to coach 1:1 so many of you whom I met in workshops or while making a formal presentation. Each of you has been a gift: you trusted me and let me know that our conversations signaled a turning point in your life. As you know, confidentiality is paramount in our relationship, but don't be surprised if you think you see "you" in the universal experience of getting there and staying there. To preserve confidentiality, the stories in the book are composites.

A very special thank you to Ellen Langer for "mindfulness" and for making me laugh. And I could always count on lifting a few ideas from Father Jim Savage's homilies. Bless you, Father Jim. To Judy Habib and the gang at KHJ Brand Integration, thanks for applying your brilliant creativity to this project.

To my readers, my hope is that this book will accelerate your ability to get there and stay there. You can measure your success as I do by the rich network of friends, family and supporters who cheer you on to the goal of your choice and who are there to celebrate and share your success.

Contents

Foreword

Decades ago I argued that therapy should be broken up into two distinct roles. The first should consist of emphatically revealing to the client not only that s/he is not alone and that many people suffer in similar ways, but also all the means required to lift their depression, phobias, and anxieties. The second should be geared to living a successful life, not merely alleviating problems. Since therapists were being trained in the former, the latter went unheeded. Then, through no efforts of mine, along came this new field, coaching, to fill the gap. In my view, Priscilla Douglas's new book represents the best of what this young field has to offer.

I've been researching mindfulness without meditation as the path to well-being and success since the 70s. The issues discussed here overlap so creatively with that work that it's easy to see that not only are Priscilla's suggestions wise and experientially sound, they are largely research-based.

We live in a world mistakenly dominated by the search for absolute right answers. The result is a mindless illusion of certainty. As this book makes abundantly clear, it is asking the right questions that leads to the difference between success and failure.

There is one question or choice not covered here, about which I've written, that I offer to further the reader's success. Rather than ask "Can I do it?' (or more generally, "Can it be done?"), try asking "How can I do it?" (or more generally, "How can it be done?"). The latter bypasses insecurities and the confusion between what already exists and what is possible. In response to the question, "How can I be more successful?" the answer is straightforward: Begin by reading this book.

— *Ellen Langer*

Introduction

One's destination is never a place,
but rather a new way of looking at things.
— Henry Miller —

After four years on the job, Sonia needs to come to grips with the fact that reliable results aren't enough to assure her promotion to Managing Director. Edwin wants to make SVP before his fortieth birthday; therefore, he thinks he doesn't have time to linger over lunch. Raphael feels overlooked; he wants to break out of his research role and find a way to put his talents on display. Patrice needs to distinguish herself from her peers in order to win one of the few positions at the next level.

Like my clients, you have a goal in mind. You know what "success" looks like for you, and your aim is to move up your career ladder until you get there. But recently you have noticed that the ladder changes as you climb higher. Where once it was clearly vertical and the rungs evenly spaced and secure, now that ladder has turned into a carnival ride with slanted, missing, slippery, and moving rungs. Sometimes it's a trapeze, and you have to let go and leap to the next level. As you eye your next step, you realize that the skills that got you where you are won't get you where you want to go.

How will you *get* there? And once you attain success, what will it be like to *stay* there? This book analyzes the collective experience of people who are climbing toward the pinnacle of success as they define it for themselves: successful, competent people who are en route to the C-suite or are already established there, who have recognized that at some point the game changes. In fact, no matter where you are in your career, the skills and behaviors you perfected to reach your current level don't guarantee promotion to the next. You can't "outperform" your peers because success is no longer based on merit alone. As you approach the executive ranks, selection is based on a new criterion: *fit.* Your superiors no longer ask whether you can achieve your performance goals—*everyone* at your level delivers results and more. They ask,

"Does she have the right leadership qualities? Is he adaptable and agile? Does she represent the future of this organization? Does he *fit?*"

Let me give you an example from my own past. I got my first executive opportunity when I was relatively young. I had no clue what to expect—or what was expected of me—when I was catapulted from Manager to Director with only two levels between the CEO of a major international manufacturing company and me. In fact, I had been with the company only two and a half years; most of my colleagues in the executive suite had collected their twenty-five–year service watches. Twenty-five years is not just a measure of time; it represents a rich network of relationships, a solid foundation of "know-how"—organizational and political savvy. Over time, you acquire the skills to navigate and be in sync with the corporate culture. Twenty-five years means that you and your colleagues have shared ups and downs and can forgive one another's occasional missteps. After two and a half years I had gotten there; twenty-five years means you have stayed there for the long haul.

I took one look at my organizational setting and simply dismissed it as an "old boys' network." After all, as a young woman, I was there (unofficially) to shake things up. I was *supposed* to "look different." I did stand out from the pack, but for all the wrong reasons: I focused on "getting the job done" and didn't take the time to have lunch and build friendships. I didn't know how to seek support and feedback or cultivate allies and advocates. In senior leadership meetings, I asked questions without seeing how ill timed they were. I didn't know about socializing an idea, hashing it out before and after—not during—the meeting. I supported people, not knowing what everyone else knew about their track records. I inherited a staff, but didn't know "where the bodies were buried" and didn't know how to find out. It seemed that every step was a mishap taking me away from success instead of propelling me forward.

Everyone hits the wall at some point in his or her career, or the next rung on the ladder isn't where he or she expects it to be. You abruptly notice that your skill set, expertise, style, or approach is no longer effective. In my case, I had "gotten there" according to the org chart but not in my behavior and mindset. I didn't understand the difference between *getting there* and *staying there*. I had the knowledge, competence, and capacity to fulfill the functional responsibilities of my role, and I thought that was enough. But I lacked all the understanding and skills necessary to succeed and stay in my role. I didn't know the "right" way to get things done. I didn't know what was expected or what was appropriate and (more important) I didn't know how to find out. In the now-familiar words of Werner Erhard, "I didn't know what I didn't know." In the end I was flailing, trying everything to stay afloat, each desperate action creating more problems. I lost my confidence, I felt I couldn't do anything right, and guess what: I was right. Finally, I accepted the fact that I didn't "fit" and my career at that organization went down like the *Titanic*.

Two and a half years wasn't nearly enough time. But my problem wasn't that I needed twenty-five years on the job in order to succeed. What I needed was this book. I wish that I had had a coach early on in my career. That is one reason I became a coach.

Who is this book for?

A lot has happened since the day I packed up my desk. I went on to success in business and government and eventually brought my experience and insight to bear helping leaders and executives at all levels and in all industries. I have worked with individuals and cohorts of high-potential employees, advising men and women of all ages, shapes and colors—people like you, who are committed to professional growth and development. Like them, you are on your way to the C-suite, or you may already have landed there with a new leadership responsibility or role. Perhaps you have recently been promoted or designated as "high potential," or you are a new member of a senior leadership team. Or maybe you find yourself overlooked for promotion, or feel bored and sidelined in an executive position. Whatever your situation, you recognize that continued success requires that you refresh and realign your approach to work and to your new constellation of stakeholders.

But although you may be temporarily "stuck," you are ambitious, gifted, and highly capable. Consider these traits that all successful people have in common. If you do not meet this threshold, no amount of coaching will help you get where you want to go, or allow you to remain there when you arrive. These are the basics—the table stakes for the game.

- Competence. You have mastered the content of your role and excel at your function.
- Capacity. You take on new assignments and are open to growth.
- Credibility. You are known for delivering what you promise.
- Communications. You make your point with clarity and energy.
- Confidence. You recognize your own competence, capacity, credibility, and communications skills.

Are you agile?

Let me add another requirement: You are comfortable facing unexpected events, uncertainty, and ambiguity. Given the dynamics of today's world, you have to change your approach—update your behavior—to respond quickly and appropriately to events. It isn't optional. We have all personally experienced a tsunami of change—with more to come. At the risk of saying "I told you so," let me share part of a presentation entitled "Five Skills for the Future" that I made to the Club of Rome in 1997. Remember the context: Google was founded in 1996, social networking was in its infancy and, in the words of Dr. Deming, we were in "a new economic age."

> Strong evidence exists that the real action as it relates to learning, discovery, and interaction is on the Internet. ...The new media is reshaping learning and knowledge. ... This new system expands the boundaries of the traditional classroom and extends learning to a life-long endeavor. The new system is based on two assumptions: (1) learning is (and is likely to remain) a social activity; and (2) knowledge is the primary commodity in an information-based economy.
>
> For the first time in human history, the *capability of interconnection* has been *given to the individual*. ... The new media allow people around the world to talk to each other, share experiences, and create new ways to bridge differences. ... We are finding ways to connect, learn, and innovate. Virtual gathering places are emerging: knowledge communities, communities of practice, cyber-tribes and just plain "chat rooms."

Looking back with the benefit of hindsight, it's no surprise that the revolutions engendered by the World Wide Web and social media have caused you and your organization to change in profound ways.

You are looking forward today, and the pace of change, if anything, is accelerating. If you think you are comfortably ensconced in a senior position and don't need to participate in the latest technological changes, think again. You can't sit this one out. Just as important as being facile with current technology, you must be aware of what's coming next and savvy enough to be ready for the next generation. You must be agile, and technology is only the most obvious arena where you must develop and prove your agility; emerging economies, changing demographics and global shifts in power are but a few others. Given the pace and scope of global change, every organization and every savvy leader are trying to stay ahead of the game.

Beyond the changing external environment, your own situation is in flux. Different arrays of skills, knowledge and behaviors are necessary at different times; the accomplishments that were once considered "stretch" are now taken for granted. Yes, you have a solid track record of success: you are competent. Your peers, clients and manager trust that you will deliver; in other words, you have credibility. Your communications skills are consistent; you direct activities and follow through. However, behind closed doors, senior leaders agree that you are good—really good—but.... What's missing? You lack the mindset of the C-suite. You arrived at this stage of your career because you are competent, you can do the job. But as soon as you begin in your new role, function or organization the performance metrics change: Your "soft skills," behavior and style will determine your long-term success. And, there are different requirements for getting there and staying there.

The bottom line is that there is always a "skills gap." You may be new to a position or role, or recognize that you are in a dynamic environment with external forces demanding that you grow. No matter what your individual circumstances, expect that something will be "missing." You will discover that some areas need to be "tweaked" and other areas must change more dramatically.

How should you use this book?

This book doesn't give you the answers. It isn't a list of "how tos" and there's no answer key in the back. After all, if everyone followed the advice contained in the rows of self-help books on bookstore shelves, leaders would excel, teams would collaborate, projects would be well managed, productivity would soar and miscommunication would cease to exist. (I personally wish that I could master and manifest the "how tos" in *Think and Grow Rich.*)

Unlike books that give you the answers, this book asks you the questions. As an executive coach, I find that my clients almost always have the answers. What they don't have is a committed listener asking the hard questions. As a coaching guide to accelerate your career, *Getting There and Staying There* poses a series of questions that reveal the behaviors that make you stand out in your current position. Each of my clients brings unique skills, knowledge and experiences. I remind them that change is constant and as a result there is no one-size-fits-all right behavior. The "right" question can open a path to new actions or reveal new insights. Many of my clients remark, "I hadn't considered it from that point of view," or, "I am pleased that I talked this one through." This book offers you a chance to do just that. The questions are designed to help you explore your current behavior and navigate your organization. By spending time with these questions, you will become more aware of what you can *start* doing, *stop* doing and *continue* doing.

Because the challenges and your perspective change as your career evolves, *Getting There and Staying There* is organized in two sections that represent the cyclical processes of every successful career. "Getting There" focuses on ensuring that your skills, knowledge, and capacity are recognized and rewarded. "Staying There" is about not making the same mistake twice: to stay there you must anticipate and be alert to the predictable hurdles that are raised and gaps that open when you change roles or simply when you meet new people. In "Staying There," you will honfe in on the often-subtle gaps that prevent even the most talented people from attaining success *as they define it*. Each chapter highlights an issue that will arise in every professional's life—probably more than once. These issues are the typical "flags" that signal it is time for you to expand your perspective, update your approach or change your behavior. Imagine you are having a conversation with your coach, who is posing the questions in the chapter. You can work through the chapters in order, or you can take them on selectively as you recognize the need or gap in your own career. But you can't avoid any of the questions or the development steps implied in answering them. To get the most from this book focus on the questions, not on looking for the answers. Your goal is to create a new habit—a checklist—of questions that you consistently ask: Am I meeting expectations? What is appropriate given this situation? Am I aligned with key stakeholders? And, most importantly: Am I making the impact that I expected?

Are you ready to become more agile?

You may be familiar with the "Change" model often seen in leadership texts. But that "awareness/motivation/action" approach is insufficient for today's dynamic organizations. This book emphasizes *agility*, the ability to move and change direction and position quickly and effectively without losing control. The word calls to mind the gracefulness of a quick and nimble dancer or athlete; it connotes balance, speed, and coordination. But beyond its physical manifestations, *agility* represents the ability to think and draw conclusions quickly or astutley.

When we speak of *agile* leaders, we mean leaders who:

- Are alert and mindful, recognizing that conditions change—and noticing when they do;
- Adjust, adapting their thinking to meet the new conditions;
- Align, synching themselves, their attitudes and behaviors to the reality of their environment;
- Act, making their move appropriately.

As you work through the book, your answers to these questions should help you make the agile moves so you can be given the next position or maximize your value in your current role.

Are you **Alert**?

- Describe the gap between where you are now and what you need to succeed.

Can you **Adjust**?

- Are you willing to change?
- What is the benefit of the change?
- What do you need to adjust: skill, style, approach, process, expectations, etc.?
- Describe the "low-hanging fruit"—what can you change immediately that visibly demonstrates your commitment?
- What longer-term (4 to 6 month) change do you need to make and what resources and relationships will you need in order to make the adjustment?

Do you **Align** yourself to organizational context?

- Who will notice?
- What would be the impact and benefit to the organization?
- What are the risks and rewards?
- What is the impact on peers, co-workers etc.?
- What are the impact and benefit to family and friends?
- Are you committed to doing what is needed to align with your boss, co-workers, etc.?

Do you **Act**?

- Are you confident to take the next step?
- Do you have what you need to take action (e.g., skills, resources, credibility, support)?
- What is your immediate next step?
- Who will provide feedback or coaching?
- How will you measure results?

Do you have the courage to change?

Maybe you think you are doing everything you can, or that success will come to you if you just hang in there and keep doing what you're doing. But consider the story of Tiger Woods. Leave aside his personal life for a moment and look back on his golf career. Since first winning the Masters in 1997, Tiger Woods has reinvented his swing not once but three times. At a moment when most of us would have been popping the champagne, he reached for the next level. Watching a video of the swing that had dominated the Masters, he saw the attributes that, if uncorrected, would limit his performance in the future. He analyzed the necessary changes and undertook the unbelievably courageous task of implementing them *all at once, while he was at the top of his game.* As he would later say, "We tore it all apart and built it up." Seven years and five consecutive scoring titles later, a changed situation—injuries to his right knee—prompted him to reinvent his swing again. And again, in 2010, while ranked number 2 in the world, he undertook another major change, working on his swing in competition, in full view of the cameras and the critics. It's clear that Tiger Woods plans to continue analyzing and changing his behavior as long as he plays the game.

Like the best athletes, agile executives are *alert* and recognize what is going on, they *adjust* their thinking, they *align* themselves with the situation, then they *act*. With this attitude, you can explore and discover the actions and behavior that are uniquely appropriate for you to be more effective as a leader: to be a leader who produces the "right" results in the "right" way. Success goes to the agile!

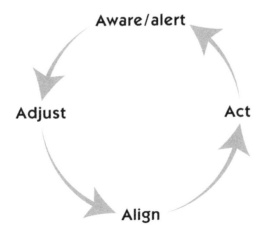

Getting There

Behavior is what a man does,
not what he thinks, feels, or believes.
— Emily Dickinson —

What is "getting there"? *Getting there* is attaining your professional objective, whether it is a new position, an interesting assignment, or a role in a project that can be the stepping stone to your next achievement.

Even though you are competent in your functional area and you are confident in your skills and abilities, your success is not guaranteed. After all, each new position requires that you master new behaviors, skills, and relationships. If you had already proven yourself in this arena, you'd already have the new role. So let's look at what may be going on if you are feeling the need to be getting somewhere.

If you feel you have achieved all you can achieve in your current position, then it is time to move. You are underutilized, and probably feel bored and maybe even resentful for being passed over. In order to make your move to your next step, you need to take action in these domains:

1 Get clarity: What do you want? Notice that I did not ask you what you *don't* want! Affirm your choice whether it is a plum project assignment, an international posting, a promotion, or simply more time for your family.

2 Link what you want to a business objective. Your desires will elicit a big yawn and "How nice for you" unless you can show how accomplishing them will move the business forward.

3 Develop the language around a strategic business conversation. Understand and use the vocabulary of the most senior people in your business.

To succeed in getting there, you need to put these pieces into place:

- Show that you understand the business by asking the right questions, using the right language, and framing your questions and comments with sound business acumen.
- Establish a good board of advisers for yourself—a group of people who will tell you the truth.
- Find someone to mentor—it will raise your visibility in the organization.
- Learn to delegate as much as possible, then delegate *more*.

The actual skills associated with getting there depend on how you define success at your current level. You must excel at the three C's before you even consider trying to get to the next level:

- Competent: you know your stuff
- Credible: you have delivered consistently over time
- Confident: you must exude confidence

Add to those basic requirements excellent communication skills and strong cross-boundary relationships.

To get to the next level, you must develop the mindset and skills of that next level and, even more important, you must create opportunities for yourself to display them. What does it take? Agility. When you are able to answer the following questions succinctly, purposefully and with confidence you are on your way to getting there: What do you want? What are your choices? Do you have the skills, network, resources? What gaps do you need to fill?

Do I Have the "Right Stuff"?

We always tend to fulfill
our own expectations of ourselves.
— Brian Tracey —

Since being promoted three years ago, Arthur had taken on projects of increasing complexity and visibility, leading cross-functional teams to successful and profitable outcomes. He worked side-by-side with his teammate Gwen for four months, researching the best solution to a big potential client's problem, and he was proud of his results. Naturally, he was thrilled when Gwen bagged the multimillion-dollar sale.

> This project is the icing on the cake! The client was more than satisfied, and the team worked together like Justin Timberlake's back-up dancers. I'm definitely ready for the division director role.

Arthur was less delighted when his boss spent three minutes praising Gwen at staff meeting, but didn't even mention the sophisticated solution that he and his team had worked so hard to come up with—the solution that made the sale possible! His mind began swirling with bits of feedback from previous situations: "You need a bit more seasoning." "I would like you to be more visible with clients." "You could do a better job getting buy-in from the folks in London." " I want to see how well you work on this project and then we can talk about next steps." Arthur's confidence was shaken.

> What's it going to take to get noticed around here? The Statler account was huge! Did the boss think Gwen developed the concept herself?

By contrast, Gwen seemed grounded and secure in her accomplishment—and she got the sales commission to prove it! Gwen publicly and appreciatively acknowledged Arthur's contribution, but somehow the message hadn't gotten around the firm. With the Statler account as his wakeup call, Arthur decided to take a new approach. Building on a workshop he had attended on personal branding, Arthur decided to take steps to highlight his importance to the organization. He found a quiet time and place away from the daily demands to consider exactly how he added value—what made him unique—to the organization.

How do you add value?

It's a common scenario: many talented people make important contributions to the success of their organizations yet fail to receive the acknowledgment and rewards they feel they deserve. Like them, you may wonder, "Does what I do matter? Does anyone even know I'm here? Do I have the right stuff?" Even though "it takes all kinds to make a world," it seems that the rainmaking sales staff is always in the spotlight.

But savvy contributors know that many crucial components add up to create success. Indeed, the ability to add value is a key metric of performance for every function in a successful organization. Developing and demonstrating the knowledge and capacity to contribute to the firm's success are essential prerequisites to advancement. That's why the starting point of this conversation is an honest personal assessment of your contributions.

1 The first step is to confirm that you are **competent**. Competent means that you have the technical know-how and a specific expertise. It is the "stuff" that landed you in the organization in the first place. Competence is the absolute minimum achievement necessary to retain your position, let alone move beyond it. If you are reaching for that next level, it is not only essential that you be viewed as competent, but also you must demonstrate abilities beyond the requirements of your current role.

2 You have **credibility** with your manager, peers and clients. You don't just do what you say you are going to do, when you say you are going to do it—you often delight your clients by your unique approach. Your word is your bond and when you make a promise to deliver your co-workers and clients can take that promise to the bank. Your most recent 360-degree feedback instrument gives you insights on how your teamwork or leadership style is perceived by your peers, key clients and your superiors. Take this information seriously: The perceptions of all these groups make up your reputation.

3 You must be skilled at cross-functional **collaboration** and **communications**. If your work spans boundaries and geographies

4

be attuned to your ability not just to meet targets but also to be respected and appreciated throughout your organization.

How do you stack up? Assign a value to each of the following (1 is low and 5 is high):

Quality	Score	Action to take
Competence: I know what I am doing	1 2 3 4 5	
Credibility: I do what I say	1 2 3 4 5	
Collaborate: I work well with others	1 2 3 4 5	
Communicate: People understand and take the appropriate action based on what I say	1 2 3 4 5	

Are you competent? Credible? An effective collaborator and communicator? If you scored low in any area, take steps to raise the level of your performance in these key qualities. If you are not scoring 5s across the board, you have work to do to gain the "right stuff." Complete the chart with actions you can take to effectively raise your score. After an honest self-assessment, Arthur outlined some action steps for himself.

What makes you unique?

Arthur and Gwen are both viewed as smart and hard working. However, hard work is not enough to get to the next level. In fact, "He's a hard worker" becomes a catch-all phrase that can obscure the unique skill, talent, and approach that differentiate your work from that of your peers. To uncover what makes you unique consider the following:

1 What is your reputation?
2 Who seeks your advice and input? Why?
3 How do your friends, peers, co-workers describe you?
4 Why did your manager hire you?
5 How do you feel when people recognize your talent and skill?

Notice that I am not asking you what *you* think about yourself. I'm suggesting you take an "outside-in" view in order to discover what *others* think is your value. And don't ignore the feedback from your spouse or significant other. They have the opportunity "24/7" to observe your strengths and unique capabilities.

For example, Linda's expertise in sickle cell anemia has led to her being sought out by the National Institute of Health. She is heading a national study and will present a report to the American Medical Association next year. However, when she was asked to take a leadership role at her hospital, she wondered, "Why me?" That is the wrong question! It is more useful to see yourself from the other person's point of view. Linda's division head sees her as a recognized expert in quality improvement; the National Institute of Health sees her as a thought leader and innovator; her colleagues view her as passionate and patient-centric, and her brother considers her to be a "Rock of Gibraltar" and the heart of the family.

The gap in perception is between Linda and Linda, not among her wide circle of advisors. Does she have the right stuff to reach the next level? Yes, but....

Closing the Gap

I often remind my clients that when they ask themselves "yes or no" questions about their abilities, the answer is almost always a resounding "No." "Do I have the right stuff?" is just such a question. It is much easier to see what's wrong with ourselves than it is to recognize all the things that are not only "right" but also valued by others. Seeing what is "right" is especially challenging if you are a self-described perfectionist caught up in the cycle of always moving the bar and forever falling short. So re-think the question and change it from "Do I have the 'right stuff'?" to "What's 'right' about me?" Now you are ready to focus on the areas in which you can shine.

To accelerate your move to the next level, leverage your strengths—your unique skills and talents. Your talents will open the door to the next opportunities, but focusing on your weakness will close your eyes to possibilities. As you climb the ladder, choose to be elevated by your strengths and see your future as "half full." If you climb the ladder weighed down by all the things you think you are not good at, you will surely see the glass as "half empty."

Making this mental shift of seeing yourself from the other person's point of view is not easy—it requires attention and practice. That's why your personal marketing campaign will help keep you on course.

How do you answer "Tell me about yourself"?

Bringing your perceptions in line with those of your manager, co-workers and spouse will take practice. I recommend that my clients craft a sound byte to capture and communicate their unique talents. Even if you haven't formulated it in words, you contribute to your organization in a way that is all your own. To understand your unique skills and capabilities start by asking yourself and others a series of questions designed to uncover what makes you unique:

- What am I known for? Sum it up in a few words or a sentence, creating a sound byte for yourself: "I align, lead, and successfully manage cross-functional teams." "I'm the go-to guy for delicate negotiations."
- What am I most proud of? What particular accomplishment stands out? Arthur quickly answered, "I developed the solution that enabled us to win the Statler account."
- What makes me stand out from my peers? Sometimes a combination of traits is particularly valuable. "I'm an engineer with excellent team and people skills."

After you have answered these questions for yourself, ask some trusted advisors for their responses. They may give you insights or ideas you hadn't considered. Is the feedback consistent with what you consider to be your strengths? Consider the feedback carefully: At the very least it represents part of your reputation.

Prepare in advance and write your answers down so that when people say "Tell me about yourself" you have a ready response. Here are a few more examples:

- I love solving problems
- I think outside the box
- I am passionate about…
- I am interested in…
- I enjoy….

And, if you are reluctant to talk about yourself, you can begin in one of these ways:

- People describe me as ….
- People come to me for…
- My key client thanked me for….
- As team lead, I ….

Note that the sentences begin with *I* and not with *We*. Beginning with *I* may make you cringe, especially if you are describing what you accomplished as a member of a team or as a team leader. Stop cringing and remember the purpose of the exercise: You are marketing *your* role, *your* unique skills, *your* specific contribution and *your* accomplishment distinct from that of the whole team. When someone asks *you* a question, it is good form to answer it directly with *I*, not the "royal we."

Remember that it will take practice before you can market your unique skills and talents with confidence and authenticity. If you are still reluctant to begin with *I,* you can always close by following Gwen's example: Thanking Arthur for his role, and communicating how proud she is to be a member of a successful team.

Take a moment now to write down three sound bytes and practice saying them. Practice first in front of the mirror, then to your spouse or significant other; finally, try out a few at work.

Is there a C-suite mindset?

Your capacities and knowledge are the cornerstones of your success, but they play only a part in advancing your career. They are necessary, but not sufficient; they let you in the game but don't assure your victory. You have confirmed that you add value by more than meeting the requirements of your role, and you have analyzed the qualities that make you stand out from others. But you can't add value in a vacuum. You must link your contribution to a business objective. You must do something well *and* it must add value to the bottom line.

Now consider how your abilities play in your environment. Context is everything—the best fastball in the world is useless in bowling! Within your organization, you must display several key qualities:

- Business acumen. Do you know what makes the business tick? What are the major deliverables or milestones that control the ebb and flow of the business, and how do you fit in? What "levers of control" are at management's disposal? How is your organization structured, and why? Who are the key players, and who makes the key decisions?
- Organizational savvy. How does your organization really work? Is the environment entrepreneurial and innovative, welcoming ideas and input from the ranks, or does a top-down hierarchy determine every decision and move? Does one person or group hold power beyond what is shown by the organizational chart? What causes people to fail or be sidelined? Do people recover from set-backs? How? What *must* you do to be successful—display leadership? Gain particular experience? Develop relationships? Conform to a set image?

C-Suite Mindset
BLOOM WHERE YOU ARE PLANTED
Advisor: Yvonne Jackson
Former Chair of the Board, Spelman College

I believe in the law of attraction. If you are clear about your goals and where you are headed you will build support systems that inform and nourish you. The support systems allow you to stay connected. When I think about my early career, I see that I owe my success to the fact that I have always worked harder and more strategically than the people around me. When I was an executive recruiter at Avon, I was responsible for the technical area—engineers, metallurgical engineers. I remember going to the VP of the area—it was a bold move—and saying, "You have five people working for you and they are all requesting people. I want to get everyone in the room to see if there are differences." To my surprise, the VP said, "I will get them in the room." That move signaled the beginning of a relationship that remains strong to this day. It was a routine job that I approached strategically. Some people may have even viewed it as not important, but I valued what I was doing and I valued the people who worked around me. I treated what I was doing as the ultimate—the most important work that I could be doing. I never denigrated the work I was doing or its contribution to the enterprise. Of course I had aspirations, but every time I got promoted I was surprised because I was always focused on what I was doing. I always did the best at what I was doing. Bloom where you are planted.

- Culture. The unwritten rules are more important than the published policies—they are "how we do things around here." Is the culture one of easy give and take, where the open exchange of ideas and disagreement are welcomed? Or is everyone expected to fall into lockstep with the plan without pointing out its pitfalls? Does the culture embrace diversity in opinions and contributions as well as in race and gender?

If you don't fully understand the ecosystem in which you are operating, you may add value but it will never be noticed or acknowledged.

Approach learning about the business, your organization and its culture as you would approach learning a new language: pay attention, be curious, and experiment. Take advantage of a mentor who has made the transition into a senior position and knows how to "navigate" the system.

How can you share your value?

Being successful is one thing; being recognized for the value that you bring is another. The extent to which you are known determines your value. Value and visibility go together. Besides understanding *what* you bring to the party, you must know *who* in the organization values your contribution and why. Then you must communicate your "value-add" in order to get the outcome you desire.

Think again about the sound byte you developed earlier. Take some time to refine it, so that you are comfortable using it when you are introducing yourself. For example, "I'm Arthur Blank. I led the team that developed the Statler solution last quarter." "I'm Stella Michaels from Legal. I'm just coming off the Widget patent case, which I'm happy to say was resolved in our favor." Many people are uncomfortable with self-promotion. They don't want be seen as a person who brags or who takes credit for the accomplishments of others. Remember: There is a big difference between "selling" and "telling." If you perform real work of genuine value, you aren't boasting when you mention your success. If you are one of those quiet types who are waiting to be noticed, you may end up waiting forever. My question to you is, *if you don't talk about who you are and what you have accomplished, who will?*

Create opportunities to contribute and put your skill, knowledge, or experience to use. You want to demonstrate that you are capable of the next level, so find or create an opportunity to display your abilities. One path that Arthur took was to get himself on the calendar of an upcoming in-house knowledge-sharing conference with a presentation on "Finding Creative Solutions to Customer Challenges."

Consider your cross-functional exposure. Does your network extend to other divisions and across levels? Volunteer or get assigned to cross-functional task forces and teams. Let others throughout the organization experience how much you add to any effort you are part of. Solid relationships that span the organization are key to your success.

Your network of friends, colleagues, and clients is your most important marketing vehicle. What they say about you largely defines your reputation—and ultimately determines the value of your personal brand. So nurture your network consciously. Reach out, help them whenever you can, and keep in touch.

Advocate for self? Really?

Activate your network: Get out there and spread the word. Be an advocate with the point of view of telling, not selling. Speak of your accomplishments with visible pride, knowledge, and personal accountability. When you communicate with pride, you reinforce your competence and display confidence. The depth of your knowledge establishes your credibility. By taking ownership—"I led the team"—you convey your value-add to the business. If you want to get ahead, start marketing your accomplishments with justifiable pride—not arrogance, exaggeration or embellishment—and give yourself the credit you deserve. Don't sit back and expect your boss to be your public relations person. At your level, your future is up to you.

What are your next steps?

What adjustments do you need to make now to ensure that you have the right stuff to excel in your current role and be viewed as ready for the next level? How quickly will your efforts be recognized? Focus on the *what*: your competence and credibility and the *how*: communication and collaboration. Add your thoughts and ideas below. Remember: to ensure a string of successes, always begin by picking the low-hanging fruit. What are the actions you can take *now*?

	Complete the Following	Low-Hanging Fruit
ALERT?	Key competencies are... My reputation... Skills/talents my boss values are...	

ADJUST?	• I lack confidence when...
	• I am reluctant to advocate/
	  market my accomplishments
	  because...	

ALIGN?	• My co-workers value... • My clients value... • My manager values...	

ACT?	• List the sound bytes that reinforce
	  and communicate my unique
	  skills and talents...
	• Identify opportunities to advocate
	  for myself...	

2

What Am I Missing?

The world loves talent but pays off on character.
— John W. Gardner —

After his boss left the company to join a competitive firm, for the first time in his career Will found himself with a manager he didn't know. He was accustomed to being hand-picked for assignments and he took pride in his reputation for being easy to get along with. But now Will was dissatisfied with his relationship with his manager. Over the past months, she had assigned several promising new accounts to his peers, but none to him. This fueled his anxiety about how she would rate his performance in the company's forced ranking system and whether she would recommend him for promotion to the next level. Will believed he deserved the highest rating, and raised the issue in one of his regular meetings.

> I started with "It has been a wonderful year," and focused on my accomplishments. I wanted to have a clear discussion about my rating, which has always been the highest—a "one." I asked, "If you had to rate my performance to date, can you give me a ball park number?" She said she hadn't put much thought to it.
>
> I was thrown off. She didn't answer my question. She said, "I'll base it on productivity, feedback from clients, and feedback from the syndicate desk. But the process won't get going until late in the fourth quarter. In the meantime, you might want to put something together regarding how you performed." I thought, "I sent that to you in advance of this meeting."
>
> I feel like I'm in a total chicken-and-egg situation. How can I get the best rating and show her I'm ready for promotion

if she won't give me any good accounts? She's not being fair or even giving me a chance. I walked away, saying, "I'll get back to you." I even thought about leaving the firm.

Will was focused on the wrong things. Trying to guess his performance rating now was a bit like checking next week's dinner menu on the *Titanic*. He hadn't even thought about *why* he wasn't being assigned the plum accounts. He only suspected that he wasn't meeting his boss's expectations and that something was missing in his performance as well as in their relationship. He wasn't getting answers, and it felt really personal to him. He missed the straight and easy conversations and feedback he had enjoyed with his former boss.

When you are not meeting expectations, you must ask yourself, "Am I seeing the whole picture?" and, since the answer is almost always *no*, ask, "What am I missing?" "Are my emotions keeping me from seeing (and thinking) straight?" How can Will have a rational conversation when he is so clearly upset? And how can he have a strategic conversation with his manager about what he wants when he is missing so much key information?

What information are you missing?

It's easy to miss vital information or inputs when you are concentrating on the next step and not meeting current expectations. You may be focusing on some things to the exclusion of others, or looking at the wrong things altogether. The familiar and amusing "dancing gorilla" perception experiment illustrates this point. This short video shows a group of people passing a basketball back and forth; when asked to count the passes, subjects actually *did not see* a person in a gorilla suit dancing on the court because they were so focused on counting passes! When you are intensely focused on one thing, it's easy to miss other information, especially if it doesn't support your point of view.

Or perhaps you aren't listening to the right people, or asking the right questions. When I served as White House Fellow and Special Assistant to William H. Webster, Director of the Federal Bureau of Investigation, I learned the importance of asking thoughtful or pointed questions. Judge Webster always seemed to ask the one question that opened up a new way of viewing a situation or exposing a flaw in a trail of logic. His questions came from a perspective that encompassed the whole of the action. By contrast, most people ask questions that merely nibble at the edges of a situation.

When you don't ask the right question, you see only a small part of the answer. When faced with a problem, many people start by asking, "What's wrong?"

Are you focusing on "what's wrong?"

Maybe you are meeting a client for the first time and struggling to find a way to connect. Or, like Will, you are concerned that your boss is short-changing you by not assigning you more lucrative accounts. Or, compared to your peers, you think you lack influence with your seniors. In any of these situations, it's all too easy to ask yourself "What's wrong?" When I was floundering in an early assignment, I asked every possible version of "What's wrong?" What's wrong with them? It's an old-boy network! What's wrong with this company? They're stuck in the past! I finally settled on "What's wrong with *me?*" Let me tell you, lingering on that question is one great way to destroy your confidence!

In fact, I'd like to wrap all these "wrong" questions with yellow CAUTION tape! These questions don't lead to awareness and action; instead, they will take you down rat holes of blame and self-doubt. You may think that there is something wrong with *you*, something wrong with *them*—your manager or colleagues—or something wrong with *it*—your group, division or the entire company. You may even have evidence supporting your view. Maybe it *is* an old-boys' network. Maybe the organization *should* have provided you with an effective mentor or coach. So what?

You can waste precious time trying to figure out what is wrong out there and apportioning blame appropriately. Consider my client Sophia who, eighteen months after being promoted to Director of Recruiting at the age of 28, felt swamped by mounting responsibilities.

> It seems like more gets added to my plate every day—and of course nothing ever gets taken off! Don't misunderstand me. I love my job—at least I thought I would, but....

When I hear the word *but*, it is like hearing a train whistle. Sure enough, here comes "what's wrong":

> ... but I feel like I can't even get my head above water to see where I am going. It seems all I do is work, and the demands never stop. I never get to sink my teeth into the new initiatives I want to launch—that I was hired to implement. There must be more to life than putting out fires. My friends are married

or have moved away. I lost my grandmother and my uncle this year and frankly I didn't think my life would be like this. I thought I'd be married with kids, not drowning in work. Sorry, I didn't expect to cry.

"What's wrong?" kicks off a predictable line of thinking. When you ask, "What's wrong?" the answer is usually loud and clear, "Yes, as a matter of fact, there is something really wrong—with you!" Psychologists refer to this as the inner voice or self talk, or I use a more colorful term: it's Rasputin speaking. Whatever you call it, that voice is rarely telling you what a great person you are, job well done! No, its role is to state the familiar and the obvious, "Yep, it's your fault, dummy. You aren't measuring up."

"What's wrong?" led Sophia to think that something was wrong with her work situation *and* with her. She had moved up to a new role, carrying the expectations of her old role with her. Unable to see what was different about her new role, she failed to prioritize or delegate effectively. She concluded that her future would be filled with more work and, to make matters worse, she now believed that her career had displaced her opportunities for marital happiness. Her expectation was framed as a zero sum game: work or happiness.

What are you missing?

A much more useful question is "What am I missing?" When the conversation shifted to "What are you missing in your work situation?" a different picture emerged. Sophia wasn't just buried under busy work—her role was packed with growth potential.

> Actually, this would be a great job if I could tame my need to have everything be perfect. I have a lot of freedom and creativity in my work. I've been widely recognized for one of my projects. The new assignment is broadening my experience and I can use it to round out my resume. Oh, I forgot to tell you—I joined a new professional group and I am meeting a lot of great new people. I do notice that most of my peers seem to be better than me at managing their workloads. I wonder how they do it?

Unable to see the forest for the trees, Sophia had seen only the obstacles posed by each unfinished task on her desk. In doing so, she was in danger of failing to meet the broader expectations of her new role.

When she stepped back to look at the big picture, her thinking led her in an entirely new direction, away from things that "couldn't be fixed" and towards a more constructive view that could be a springboard for action. She paused (see Chapter 16) and reflected on her priorities. She sought the advice of her mentor. She revised her staffing plan.

It's OK if you can't resist your first instinct to ask "what's wrong." Just *notice* the question you start with and then *quickly substitute* one that can help you uncover new options for action. How quickly can you zero in on "What am I missing?" Your quickness signals your agility. Just as the question "What's wrong...?" assumes that something is wrong, the question "What am I missing?" assumes that there is more to be learned. When you ask "What am I missing?" you open yourself to new information, different perspectives, and fresh insights. This powerful question invites you to see the situation anew, from a fresh perspective. When Sophia incorporated a new perspective, her attitude and behavior naturally fell into alignment with it.

> The greatest obstacle to discovery is not ignorance
> —it is the illusion of knowledge.
> *Daniel J. Boorstin*

Scholar Ellen Langer popularized the concept of *mindfulness*, her work moving from research to practical applications in everyday life. Langer describes mindfulness as the process of actively noticing new things, relinquishing preconceived mindsets, and then acting on the new observations. Much of the time, she says, our behavior is mind*less*, the automatic reactions to social and cultural cues. Mindlessness blinds us to new possibilities, says Langer, and that is what drove her to study its flip side. Asking, "What am I missing?" is a step towards mindfully examining your situation. It puts the spotlight on how you interpret and engage with your situation; how you relate and respond to your context and, in sum, your expectations about your role, your organization, or your manager.

Are you mindful about your situation?

"What's wrong?" can derail your career. Will was so convinced that something was wrong that he was ready to give up. Frustrated by the lack of feedback and the possibility of a low performance score, Will continued to focus on "what's wrong":

> As the days went by, I reviewed the various accounts that other people cover. The accounts are not evenly distributed. I even asked her for better accounts. After all, other people have

received new accounts and I haven't gotten any in a while. She just said, "You can talk to me about any concerns that you have." All I want is a chance to get my performance across.

Will probably has a good handle on the "facts." His peers may indeed have more productive accounts. But raising this with his manager—pointing it out as "what's wrong"—hasn't proven particularly effective. During our coaching call, I encouraged Will to ask himself, "What am I missing?" We discovered that he was missing a lot! Amazingly, he hadn't noticed or accounted for his own attitude. Will didn't really trust his manager with his future. While he didn't think she would go so far as to throw him under the bus, he just didn't trust her. And that lack of trust was straining the relationship, making it even worse. He was giving a strong "one-foot-out-the-door" vibe—would you give *your* best accounts to someone with that attitude?

Even more important, Will's boss was clearly looking for something *else* from him, something different from what he had been doing to date. Remember Yvonne Jackson's advice in Chapter 1—"bloom where you are planted"—always do your current job exceptionally well, and go beyond expectations. Will hadn't noticed that the game had changed and the new boss had moved the goal posts. Will's boss was withholding additional assignments until he proved capable of handling them to meet *her* standards. Will was "missing" an understanding and mastery of his boss's requirements.

Here are a few insights he gained from reflecting on the situation from different perspectives.

I am very loyal—if I feel respected and rewarded. But I feel threatened by this—I don't feel like I have a chance to prove myself. So I've gotten pushy and pushed her into a corner. I need to remember that my manager hasn't given me any reason to mistrust her or believe she doesn't have my success in mind. So I have to stick to the facts, and give my trust if the facts dictate that the person is trustworthy.

I need to work on this relationship and take responsibility for improving it. I see that I am not building the relationship internally and my focus on accounts is too narrow to get ahead. I need to build a network of support. Most of all, I need to treat my manager like an internal client.

I need to understand how she defines success and pursue that as my objective.

C-Suite Mindset

BREAK FROM THE ROUTINE

Advisor: James "Chips" Stewart
Director of Public Safety and Security, Retired Chief of Detectives,
Oakland Police Department, Oakland, California

If everything is routine, you don't have a chance to show your skills. Only in the moments of sheer panic can you show yourself. If you haven't prepared, you will not succeed. Taking initiative involves risk and you have to reach beyond your comfort zone. Opportunities may or may not be present—you have to be willing to nominate yourself or volunteer for extra work to build your credentials or to get the assignment you want. In my case, I had to be willing to try some stuff in areas where I was barely qualified to do anything—to see if my skills resonated with what needed to be done.

Too many people wait to be tapped on the shoulder; some people think that if they sit up straight in their chair someone will reach down and pick them up. Getting there means looking at all the opportunities. If all of the chairs above you are filled—reassess and consider another track. And remember the words of Louis Pasteur: Luck favors the prepared mind.

It takes courage to ask, "What am I missing" and to then engage in a conversation of discovery. To change his approach from "What's wrong?" to "What am I missing?" Will divided the question into three parts:

1 *What is going on? What is the observable behavior?*
   - My manager is new—we don't really know one another.
   - My manager believes that the accounts are assigned for success.
   - My manager doesn't know me.

2 *How do I "feel" about what is going on?*
   - I don't trust my manager.
   - I am treating her "coldly."

3 *What new choice(s) can I make?*
   - Build the relationship; if I invest more in this relationship I will understand her thinking and perhaps gain her support.

- Focus on the big picture; try to see why she has allocated the accounts the way she has.
- Let her know I am on her team. Show her, not tell her, that I can do more.

Will didn't come up with all the answers on the first day, but at least he started asking the right questions. He spoke frankly with his manager about how he could be a more successful member of her team. Their relationship began to improve. Over the next few months, Will was able to frame a strategic conversation with her about what they both wanted to achieve. He was awarded more accounts and got the chance to strut his stuff, putting him in line for a high performance rating and a possible promotion.

Is there something else going on?

People often "miss" what's happening when the real action is occurring below the surface, or one event or circumstance is obscuring another. You have probably seen this warning posted at railroad crossings: "One train may hide another." It's the second train that you need to be concerned about! It may be bigger or traveling faster than the one you can see. Here's how Edith learned the lesson of looking beyond the obvious. Her hands full with new responsibilities stemming from her company's reorganization, Edith hardly noticed some big changes "hiding behind" the restructuring.

> I was so focused on my new team—looking "down"—that I hardly glanced "up"! My boss was pregnant, and she was planning to be out for four months and part-time for six months after that. It was a huge opportunity for me to show my capabilities, and I almost missed my chance to prepare for it!

Remember: Even when things seem to be going smoothly, you should always be alert to what you may be missing!

How quickly do you need to change?

> There is at least one point in the history of any company
> when you have to change dramatically to rise to the next
> performance level. Miss the moment and you start to decline.
> *Andrew Grove, Intel*

Andy Grove's statement holds true for individuals as well as organizations. No matter what you are missing—information on your role, better perspective on your manager, or your own shortcomings—it will cause problems for you. When you gain a broader perspective and fill in the missing elements, you will be able to adjust your attitude and your approach to succeed in the situation. When it comes to adjusting your behavior, my advice is always to focus on *choice*, not *change*. Change can feel daunting or make you feel like you are losing something. Focusing on *change* can cause you to dwell on "what's wrong." Focus instead on the many choices available to you. Select the ones that will move you toward your goals.

Moving quickly to address the situation demonstrates your *agility*. You don't have to be perfect or get it "right" the first time—just moving in the right direction communicates to senior managers that you are committed. You heard the feedback and took it to heart. You are open to change. These are the messages management wants to hear.

Start looking for what you are missing now.

	Complete the Following	Low-Hanging Fruit
ALERT?	• What are the facts—the observable and tangible behavior? • What are the different perspectives at play? • How has the "context" changed?	
ADJUST?	• Am I reacting emotionally? • I've seen what's wrong—but what's *right* about this situation?	
ALIGN?	• What is the gap in perspectives?	
ACT?	• What do I want? • What new choices, options, and pathways are available to achieve my goal?	

3

Do I Have the Right Circle of Friends and Colleagues?

It's the friends you can call up at 4 a.m. that matter
— Marlene Dietrich —

I took up skiing to meet people—specifically men—and as a beginner I found plenty of people to ski with on the "green" runs. Many were more experienced and willing to share tips and techniques. When you are starting out in almost any pursuit, it's easy to find people who know more than you and who are eager to help you. In most sports—running, golf, sailing, cycling—the activity spills over into socializing after the event. At the foot of the hill, the gear comes off, hands warm and formalities disappear as the day's runs are retold and embellished in après ski chatter. New friendships are easy to make. I found myself with the "right" people—a full circle of friends to ski with at my level.

By my second season I was comfortable skiing the green slopes and realized that I could excel at skiing if I worked at it. So instead of relying on my fellow-beginner friends for coaching and tips, I registered for formal lessons each time I skied. I invited others to join me, but most of my friends seemed content to ski what they already knew how to ski. I advanced steadily from green to blue to black and eventually developed a love for bump and powder skiing. It seemed that the more skillful I became, the fewer people I had to ski with. I thought, "This is ironic—I took up skiing to meet people and ended up skiing away from them!"

Eventually, I found a new group—it was smaller but "right" for me. Members of my new circle shared my passion and energy level and—importantly—they skied better than me. I became a better skier because of them. They and my instructors (I continued with formal ski lessons) encouraged me and helped me build the skills to conquer challenging terrain. But my story doesn't end there. The good news: old and new friends still get together for après ski. No one is left out, because we all love to ski.

What is the "right" circle of friends?

My experiences on the slopes provide an analogy to the way things work as you build your network and career. Some of your colleagues and friends are content where they are; some have reached a plateau, limited by their skills, style, stage of life, or level of ambition. Some want to push to the limits of their possibilities, and others are already masters of their game. All have a place in your circle, but you must understand the role each one can play at every stage of your career.

The "right" circle for you depends on you, your current situation and your desires and ambitions. You have to decide what you want and, more to the point, what is best for you (and your family) at this stage of your career. The color scheme that designates levels of skiing serves as a good way to define career stages:

- Green (Beginner): Getting started
- Blue (Intermediate): Proving yourself
- Black Diamond (Expert): Meeting the competitive challenge

And let's add a new category because sometimes we get our lift ticket pulled or we ski out of bounds:

- Time out

Are you on your career's beginner slopes?

If you are getting started, then make sure your circle includes people with knowledge and experience who will be willing to develop you and able to point out the rough spots you are sure to encounter. Engage with people who have proven expertise and who know how to transfer knowledge. Drawing from the skiing analogy, it doesn't help much if the "expert" is only slightly better than you. Your advisors should be dramatically better than you to help you avoid accidents, catch you if you fall, and show you the techniques you need to get back up.

If you are new to skiing, you can expect to move fairly quickly from the bunny slope to your first chair lift, to a short green run, and to a longer green run. When you are starting your career, develop a "Green Circle" analogous to the people you would meet on the slopes as a beginner. The folks in your orientation cohort can become key members of your circle as you learn together how to succeed in your organization. Your hiring manager will hold you accountable for meeting your job requirements and provide important feedback; your human resource contacts will connect you to professional development opportunities. Your Green Circle also includes people from your former employer or your most recent organization (college, armed services, etc.). Keep them up to date on your career's progression.

Your Green Circle will include people with different perspectives and different experience levels:

- Mentors
- Co-workers
- Hiring manager
- Human Resources professional
- Colleagues from your previous employer or college
- Role models—experts in your field that you follow via blog or online courses

Who will help you meet the challenge of the next level?

Like intermediate skiers, midlevel managers have the techniques to manage and deliver in consistent or predicable conditions, but they don't have the breadth of experience to make them fully confident in ambiguous or novel situations. In ski terms, their technique may fall apart when they find themselves on steep slopes or deep powder. At this "Blue" or intermediate level, you know which conditions cause you to be unsteady or lose confidence, and the people in your circle can help you gain the skills you need to succeed. If you are proving yourself, feedback is key, so seek insight and feedback from your boss, colleagues and friends. Your circle must include a colleague or manager who is willing to review important documents you write or give you specific feedback on your presentation style or interactions with a client. The more pointed and actionable the feedback, the more quickly you can adjust or tweak your approach.

One way to be sure you have the right people in your circle is to examine your performance measures and expectations. Just as a skier knows that success on the Blue runs requires turning, stopping and the ability to manage some icy patches, so you should define the professional abilities you want to demonstrate in order to move up. To succeed, you will probably fall short or you may even fall down a few times before you are able to be consistent. Put yourself to the test and show off your skills. The "right" circle will be able to help you connect the dots between previous performance and successes and what you need to exhibit now. Members of the "right" circle will encourage you to close the gaps in your performance, but they will not expect you to change yourself wholesale—remember: I recommend tweaking and adjusting, not a lobotomy. If your circle has breadth and depth of experience, it can guide, teach and provide feedback for the long haul as you progress through all the different levels of "Blue," all the way up to advanced intermediate.

As you move up in your career and select new members of your circle, remember the après-ski camaraderie. Creating a new circle doesn't mean that you abandon your old friends, move away, or leave them behind. If you turn your back on your old friends in skiing you will merely be seen as a cad, but this behavior in business can have long-term repercussions. A friend scorned is a former friend who may resent or even retaliate. Given the prevalence of social media and the importance of your image and personal brand, avoid the mistake of having your "friends" feel like stepping-stones. Although your interests may have diverged as you moved to the next level, there are good reasons to keep old friends in your wider circle. First, they serve as bridges to others, whether friends on the slopes or in other departments in the organization. Second, they now give you an opportunity to share what you have learned, serving as an advisor or mentor to them as others have served to you.

Your Blue circle will include:

- Your manager
- Cross-boundary or cross-organization colleagues
- Clients and customers
- Mentors
- Colleagues from professional organizations and/or charitable work
- People with different perspectives and different experience levels and,
- People who currently hold the role or have the skills that you aspire to reach.

Do you want to take on the "Black Diamonds"?

Not everyone aspires to ski black diamond runs. The terrain is variable and requires mastery and agility. Skiers at this level are aware of what they can and cannot ski; they take responsibility for themselves and, by extension, for others.

Of course, there are different levels of black diamond skiers and when my friends Kirk Sykes and Billy Biscoe say, "Let's hike up there so we can jump in," I say, "See you at happy hour!" The "right" circle will respect your decision and offer advice or techniques so you will be able to ski with them the next time. Your circle—especially your manager—will provide stretch opportunities that take you out of your comfort zone. It's up to you to signal that you are ready and to have the right circle of resources to succeed. Remember how I continued with formal lessons as I progressed as a skier? Your formal relationship with a coach or mentor serves the same purpose.

Think about the connections within your circle. You have left the crowded intermediate slopes and you are one of the few skiing a tree-lined run. You have taken an assignment that is challenging in all the right ways. You have the right circle for success: trusted advisors with the right mix of expertise and temperaments, at least one person with the history—who knows the terrain—and someone who will shout a warning so you don't crash or go out of bounds. Your Black Diamond group will include:

- Your manager
- Your manager's manager
- Customers and clients
- Board members and members of professional organizations
- Colleagues in your group and across organizational boundaries
- External advisor or coach
- Your spouse or significant other
- People you admire and people who inspire you

Your current circle is no more than one person removed from the resources or information that you need. As a result of this proximity, you will have *access*; you will be able to use your influence to get things done. Once mobilized, these connections will accelerate your ability to navigate new terrain and take on bigger projects; because your trusted friends and allies have your back, you can step out of your comfort zone with confidence.

Are you ready to compete?

Unlike in skiing, where there is usually plenty of snow for everyone, success in organizations sooner or later will involve competing for a small number of higher positions. You will have to prove yourself—skillfully display your capabilities and competencies—many times over the course of your career. The necessity to compete may appear unexpectedly if you are in a new situation, whether you have accepted a new position, you find yourself being "acquired" in a merger, or you simply have a new manager.

A seasoned and experienced producer, Stephan resented having to prove himself in his new situation. He missed the ease and rapport he experienced at his previous firm:

> Back in the "old days"—just last year—we had so much fun working together. We were like peas in a pod. But everything has changed now. Our old boss is gone. He had put me in for a promotion before all this happened. Now I don't know where I stand on the promotion track—which is very frustrating. I'm back at square one, with a new boss, a whole new management team that doesn't know the value I bring. I am hoping that the year will end well —with me having succeeded despite having fewer resources. Face it, I make my boss look good and I have never been one to ask—but I am making noise now. I've got to showcase my credibility, experience, and the fact that I offer a more institutional viewpoint.

Getting there requires ambition and along the way you will encounter competition, even in a team or collaborative environment. Your goal is to contribute your skill, knowledge and expertise to meet the competitive challenge and this is where your hard work and intellect come into play. There are no short cuts—especially when it is the first time you take the lead presenting to a client or your manager has asked you to develop a project management plan. Seek out challenging opportunities that align with your skill set; in other words, go beyond your job description. Your circle will include cross-boundary or cross-organizational colleagues who share the same interests and passion, or see similar opportunities to enhance the business. Your manager and your manager's manager are likely to be involved because you are working on a "stretch" opportunity, one they assigned to you because they see that you have the ambition, skill and drive to contribute more to the business.

Being a star doesn't mean being a jerk. It means being someone that people look up to based on the combination of your work ethic, expertise and friendly, cooperative work style. Your circle includes present and former colleagues, customers, people who inspire and influence you. Stars shine brightly in their small corner of the universe—understand that your star will not be as prominent when you move to a new circle. You must work to acquire the skills and characteristics that will let you shine in your changed environment.

In a given process or system
some people matter more than others.
Malcolm Gladwell
The Tipping Point

What if the "right" circle seems too political?

George had sought out a stretch assignment that he expected would set him up for promotion because it gave him a chance to put his capabilities and expertise on display. The assignment was recognized as a big challenge, and George succeeded with flying colors. So he was dismayed when Phil got the coveted promotion to Senior Vice President.

> Phil got ahead because he is always brown-nosing. I'm not going to do that – I hate the politics in my office.

When I asked, "Why does your boss listen to Phil?" George answered quickly, "Phil tells him what he wants to hear." Really? If you believe that, what do *you* have to say that your boss would listen to? What value can you add?

Don't make the mistake of categorizing all the behavior you don't like in your workplace as "political." Instead, expand your own political acumen by realizing that what looks like a political cabal may simply be another circle of influence—a group of people who view themselves as the "right" circle. Remember that people self-organize according to their interests and, often, their ambition. These groups become more insular if the environment is competitive, when there are limited opportunities to get to the "top," or when the bonus pool or performance ratings are capped.

If you view your situation as political, don't sit on the sidelines. Figure out who has the power—or access to the source of power—in the circle or clique. Do your homework and learn about the individual members' interests, experiences, history and values. You may decide to create a foothold in the "political" circle. There are real benefits to you if you do: you will expand your perspective, become privy to conversations that you would not have heard, and gain insight or advance knowledge of the business.

Think about the connections within your circle. Your current circle of trusted advisors and friends may have a connection to the circle that you currently avoid as "too political." So now is the time to tap your current circle's members to learn about the history, key players, sources of power and influence, and the value-add of members of the "political" circle. You will have to give up your own assessment and be willing to listen for the benefit and value the rival group offers the organization and its members. Acknowledge that you are missing something about this group, and be open to learning more.

Who's in your circle when you take a time out?

At various points in your career, life circumstances give you a time out. For example, you are out of work. When this happens, your circle of friends should be a trampoline, not a hammock. In other words, don't let your circle tell you how awful you were treated or how few opportunities are out there, or voice other opinions that cause you to spend time in the hammock. Instead, look at the folks in your circle and pick **one** for a candid and even emotional conversation. This is an opportunity to tell your whole story to a person you trust and to give vent to your emotions—have a good pity party with party hats and favors. But make certain that the party isn't an all-nighter. Set yourself firm start and stop times to be respectful of the time your friend has granted; above all, don't leave your friend bummed out and handling all the emotional "clean up." Almost everyone has had a time out or failure so ask how your friend got back on his or her feet. When prompted, most people will share their stories, and you may be surprised that the "time out" has contributed to your friend's success today. Don't miss the opportunity to gain valuable insight. Tap into the wisdom of your circle by asking.

Notice that I recommend having this conversation with **one** person. Why? You don't want to reveal your deepest darkest fears to every member of your circle. This advice may seem counterintuitive—you might think, "These are my friends, I can tell them everything." No, these are your business colleagues, advisors—this is your professional network. These are the people you will mobilize to identify your next opportunity. Your professional brand is enmeshed in your circle of friends. Always be responsible and a good steward of your image; as my good friend Katye always says, "You lost your job—not your mind."

> A real friend isn't capable of feeling sorry for you.
> *Jodi Picoult*

Your "time out" circle should include a coach or a career counselor. Include your close personal friends and your spouse or significant other also. Listen to their advice carefully—they will always begin by telling you the truth. Your response—action or inaction—will set the tone for

C-Suite Mindset

DON'T LET ANYONE TAKE YOUR SPARKLE

Advisor: Evelyn Barahona
Director of Business Development, Quality Interactions

As you are moving up you have to face the fact that certain people are not rooting for your success. In fact, sometimes you may feel as if you are in the "Game of Thrones" or some other drama of deadly competition every day, and it is very important that you don't let anyone steal your sparkle. I have mentors inside and outside my company and I take advantage of peer-to-peer mentoring, too. And I rely on my "life board of directors"—they really believe in me and provide guidance; they provide a view of reality "on the ground."

For me it all comes down to relationship management. For example, in one of my first jobs I got involved in the diversity council. As an Hispanic on the council, I had access to the CEO. Interacting with the CEO made a huge difference in my career. I learned a lot and was able to pick up on business trends and directions that I would not have had access to. I started connecting the dots and eventually I was looking at the whole picture. The skills really set me apart: I had a macro view. This perspective is especially helpful in my current role and helps me be a vital member and leader in my community.

their next response. You can wear your friends down and turn them from trampolines into hammocks, so be careful.

If you have a time out, be certain that your circle includes:

- Spouse/significant other
- Coach/career counselor
- Members of professional organizations to which you belong
- Colleagues from former job (your manager if possible)
- People who are in related industries and agencies
- Clients and customers

Remember that the right network means that you are already connected to your next opportunity. Put your network to work.

Do you know how to manage your circles?

Think about the different people you engage with. It is an interesting exercise to "map" them into circles—concentric, overlapping, touching or not—and consider what benefit you offer to and derive from each group. Here is a little quiz that will help you identify some of the members of your circle. Note: I recommend that you *do not* list your mother, father, spouse, or significant other in any of these categories.

Answer the following questions about the current people in your circle:

1 Who will answer my 4 a.m. telephone call? Name(s)
2 What "high level" person will return my call or email within 24 hours?
3 When I can't see things clearly, who helps me broaden my perspective?
4 When I am feeling down, who listens and separates the "facts" from the "feelings"?
5 Who's the person I can count on for a "wake up" or "reality check"?
6 I am inspired after a conversation with _____

Maybe you notice that your circle is very strong in some areas, yet weaker in others. Perhaps you feel you have good support at your current level, but lack the "wind at your back" for the future. There are many ways to expand or revitalize your circle. For example:

- Do something different. Take up a sport or hobby or enroll in a course.
- Get out of your comfort zone. Offer to team up with a person who has skills or expertise you admire or desire.
- Break your routine. Walk around your office and talk to people instead of sending emails; invite someone you don't know for coffee.
- Find your "tribe." Seek out people who share your interest, passion and speak your language.
- Help someone less fortunate. Volunteer in your community, or mentor a young person.

My friend Chips has a great way to keep his circle relevant and responsive. Simply put, he stays in touch.

> I used to write the names of people I met on index cards, with as many details as I could remember: interest, spouse's name,

what we talked about, and where I met them. Now I have Siri and CardMunch to make all that easier, but I still keep track of the people I know. And the important thing is, I reach out to them regularly.

What is the "right" circle for you?

When you ask, "Is this the "right" circle for me?" bring a fresh approach to your answer by remembering that circles can be concentric, over-lapping, or adjacent. You will have many circles to support your professional and personal goals. Your goal, as always, is to have the right people engaged and involved in your life at the right time—especially the one(s) who will return your 4:00 a.m. call—now that's agility! The possibilities are endless.

Add your thoughts and ideas below:

	Complete the Following	Low-Hanging Fruit
ALERT?	<ul><li>Who is in my current circle?</li><li>Where are the political or "power" bases?</li><li>Who listens to whom? Why?</li><li>Am I ready to compete?</li></ul>	
ADJUST?	<ul><li>Given my professional goals, do I have the "right" people in my circle?</li><li>Given my personal goals, do I have the "right" people?</li><li>Who should I add to my circle?</li></ul>	
ALIGN?	<ul><li>Do I have the right mix of people?</li><li>What is the gap in perspectives?</li><li>Does my circle inspire me? Or bore me?</li></ul>	
ACT?	<ul><li>Do I need to revitalize or expand?</li><li>How can I recover from a time out?</li></ul>	

4

Am I Getting the Most Out of
My Mentors, Advisors, and Advocates?

A good coach will make his players see
what they can become rather than what they are.

— Ara Parseghian —

Are you at the top of your game, working hard and contributing to important projects in your organization? Are you taking part in successful teams or critical initiatives, yet somehow you remain unnoticed, just "a member of the pack" as far as senior management is concerned? Being successful is one thing; being recognized for the value that you bring is another thing entirely. The extent to which you are known determines your value. Value and visibility go together. If you've taken care of the "value" part of the equation, your mentors, advisors, and advocates can help with the "visibility."

What is happening?

Your value is truly "in the eyes of the beholder"—your boss, team members and your boss's boss. If you are toiling unnoticed, you may need advice or help to bring your efforts to the attention of people who matter. Successful people identify, cultivate, and work closely with a small group, often called a "kitchen cabinet" or an individual's "Board of Directors." The "members" have taken an interest in you and your professional development. This group consists of peers, senior managers and executives who can offer vantage points from both inside your organization and beyond it. Getting to the next level requires the skillful and strategic "use" of your mentors, advisors and career advocates. The last is the most important of these three quite different roles. Understand them and their characteristics; you will call on each at different times to help with different issues.

What is a mentor?

A mentor is someone who embodies the qualities that you admire or aspire to. Almost by definition an older or more senior person, a mentor takes you "under his or her wing." Sometimes the relationship may feel similar to that of a teacher/student or parent/child, or the mentor may even seem like a grandparent. Many first mentors are teachers or college professors. For example, Professor Nick Buffone was my mentor in college, inspiring me with his almost encyclopedic knowledge of theater, insatiable love of books and his riveting stories of international travel. I was intrigued by his accounts of exotic people, places and cuisine. I looked up to him and, at the time, I wanted my life to mirror his. I watched, asked questions and learned from him; he encouraged me and, as a result, I discovered and now enjoy a world filled with music, beauty and countless adventures.

> A lot of people have gone further
> than they thought they could because
> someone else thought they could.
> *Unknown*

The mentoring relationship is special because the mentor sees something in you that you may not have the maturity or confidence to see in yourself. Or the mentor may see something of his or her younger self in you and recognize that, with nurturing and support, that quality will grow and blossom. For example, during my first year in the doctoral program at Harvard I was the silent one in class. You would have been silent too if you saw your classmates' last names on Harvard buildings! Everything changed when Professor David Cohen invited me for coffee and a chat after class. During that conversation I discovered that I was earning the highest grades in one of the most difficult courses offered while my venerable classmates, who I thought were weaned on these topics, were falling behind.

In a business environment, mentors help mentees stay on course by sharing perspectives, insights, and experiences. Former bosses often grow into mentor relationships but, properly speaking, a mentor is not currently in a position of direct authority over you. That authority could seriously inhibit the trusting give-and-take that characterizes a true mentor relationship. Now you may be thinking, "That can't be right. My boss spends a lot of time with me. She is investing in my development and no subject is taboo between us." Agreed, the relationships may seem similar, but remember that your manager is responsible for meeting her own business objectives as well as yours. When it comes time for performance rating and bonus allocation, even the best manager/employee relationship is tested. By contrast, a mentor can help you take the broad view and see your long-term choices in a way that respects your current situation but is not limited by it. For example, your mentor can help you sort through the discussion you want to have with your manager about your salary or about the timing to move outside your department.

Recognizing the value of positive relationships outside the chain of command, some firms have developed formal internal mentoring programs. These programs assign executives as mentors for high potential staff. Like arranged marriages, both parties must work to develop mutual trust and regard to make these pairings beneficial to both mentor and mentee. The relationship is often limited to the mentor "showing the junior person the ropes"—a worthwhile outcome in itself, nonetheless. Whether you have an "arranged" mentor, or your relationship with your personal mentor is your choice, be alert to clues that tell you the relationship isn't helping you. Like any good relationship, a positive mentorship is marked by good chemistry and trust, with easy and open communication and an atmosphere of give and take.

You don't have to like your mentor or want to be like him or her to get value from the relationship. Being paired with a mentor who differs in approach, values and even personality can add breadth to your professional style. However, if you just don't "click" or you notice that you are withholding information, if your conversations are filled with "dead air" because there's nothing to talk about, or you aren't following through on suggestions, you need to take steps to immediately and respectfully remedy the situation.

How to get the most out of your mentor? Be prepared! Be ready to respond positively to your mentor's suggestions.

- Listen and act. When your mentor makes a suggestion such as, "I think that you should talk to…", follow that advice.
- Be open and get specifics. When your mentor says, "I think that you would be good at….", say thank you and ask, "What do you see in me that suggests that to you? What should I do next to build/enhance or to be more successful at that?"

What is an advisor?

Your advisors can come from across the spectrum of your life and environments. Your circle of advisors will encompass friends, family members, former colleagues, coaches, and others. The requirements for admission to your corps of advisors are simple:

- You must respect each advisor's judgment and intelligence

- You must believe your advisors have your best interests in mind and at heart

I rely on a diverse group of advisors when I want to make a decision, recalibrate my direction or get specific input. The more diverse your circle of advisors, the better! Don't limit yourself to people who have the same background as you or who see things the same way you do. Especially, seek out people who don't always agree with you or take your side.

If you routinely opt not to follow someone's advice, it only shows that you have not selected your advisors carefully. This is a quick way to tick people off and burn bridges. Select people you know will give you good advice, even if it's not exactly what you "want" to hear. Then, when you ask for advice, be prepared to accept it or let the advisor know why you are not following the advice. Always remember that advisor/advisee is a privileged relationship. It is a two-way process—the advisors are saying yes to being available, answering your questions, taking your calls and giving you access to their networks. You must be willing to do the same for them.

Here are some key points to keep in mind when approaching your advisors:

- If you already know the answer, don't ask the question. Above all, don't fish for the advice you want to hear.
- Don't ask for advice unless you are prepared to accept it.

I learned this lesson the hard way. When I was considering applying for an important city position, the first advisor I asked said "no." Unhappy with that answer, I then asked another person and she said "yes." I followed her advice. In hindsight, the first advice was correct, but I didn't listen. I learned the hard way not to go "fishing" for the advice that tells you what you already know or want to hear.

In the process of integrating the advice you get into your decision-making, you may alter your path and only move forward on part of the suggestion. If so, close the loop. Let your advisor know either before or immediately after you take action. Don't annoy your advisors by asking them to take the time to listen to your issue and offer sincere suggestions, only to see their advice disregarded. And above all don't let them find out through the grapevine that you chose another path. Don't jeopardize these important relationships. Most of the time you will find that the advice has a profound impact on how you view the situation, the way you approach the decision or the expanded perspective you now have thanks to your conversation with your advisor.

Here is how to get the most out of your advisors:

- Be clear and have a specific question, topic or request before you seek advice.
- Consider the category of advice that you seek (e.g., transitioning from individual contributor to team manager) and match with the perspective or expertise of the advisors in your network.
- Ask yourself, "Do I know this 'advisor' well enough to have this conversation?" Are you confident that having this conversation with this person will not jeopardize your career or your reputation? Be sure to guard your personal image.
- Request a meeting and state the topic for discussion and the purpose or expected outcome. Do you want help making a decision, or to gain perspective on how the advisor handled or resolved a similar issue, career opportunity or difficult situation?
- Finally, be gracious and follow up.

What is an advocate?

If you have been focusing on getting there, you have probably relied on your boss for feedback and career advice. You may not be aware of the decision-making process for major career promotions, or even who actually makes those decisions in your organization. Once you start to notice who gets promoted and how, you can begin to think strategically about expanding your professional network to include "advocates" (also known as "sponsors").

Advocates are senior people who are in the room when decisions on promotion and career opportunities are made, who assist your career by supporting your advancement when these decisions are being discussed. You may know exactly who your advocates are. Some advocates work behind the scenes and may even be unknown to you—I was lucky enough to have the company president on my side early in my career, but I did not know the extent of her interest and support until later. Don't expect an advocate to give you a definitive answer on your career. Your advocate may give you assurances that your career will move forward, without being specific on the *how* or *when*. Don't make the mistake of pressing for specifics and putting your advocate in an uncomfortable position. In addition, you can lose points by seeming "needy" or lacking confidence. Be organizationally savvy and focus on nuances—notice what your advocate is saying and not saying.

A word of caution: even if you know your advocates, the relationship you have with them is not the informal or friendly one you have with your mentor. Respect their status and role, appreciate the access you have to them and always be prepared to make a positive impression—have your elevator speech prepared or be ready with current information about your advocate so that you can make a meaningful connection when you get the chance. Formulate your elevator speech carefully; ideally it consists of

1 An active verb (past tense): "I helped increase…" or "I led…"
2 An object that matters: "sales in my division…"
3 Significant result: "by 32 percent"
4 End by stating how you "feel" about the accomplishment: "I'm proud…"

Some people are "connected," and their sponsors may be family friends or college chums. But most people have to identify and cultivate sponsors. Here is how:

- Stay current and knowledgeable about the key leaders in your organization, especially the individuals within your chain of command or extended management team. Track their careers, presentations, and "town hall" meetings.
- Make a positive and memorable first impression when introduced to senior management at networking events or special gatherings.
- Ask thoughtful questions at town hall meetings.
- After being introduced, follow up with a thank you note that includes a reference to a comment the senior manager made, showing you understand what the comment meant or how you will put it to use.
- And remember, your manager can be your best advocate and provide opportunities for you to be visible to seniors in meaningful ways.
- To get the most out of your conversations with senior management or leaders, be respectful of their position, authority and time, but don't grovel, apologize or state the obvious with openers like "I know you are busy."

How can you use your relationships with mentors, advisors, and advocates?

Mentors, advisors, and advocates each have special roles to play in your career development. It is important to ask for the right kinds of help from each. When you make a request of a member of your "circle," be sure to approach with respect and appreciation. Be aware of ways you can reciprocate or help in return.

This chart shows the different kinds of issues you might want to address, and how to frame the conversations with mentors, advisors, or advocates.

Issue	Mentor	Advisor	Advocate
Self-awareness	What do you see in me?	How can I leverage my skills, knowledge and ability?	What I bring to the organization is. ....
Career Direction	What do you recommend?	I am thinking about x, what do you think? Or, What do I need to do to get to the next level?	I understand what x requires and I would like to describe what have I have accomplished in alignment with those goals.
Business Acumen	How do you measure success?	What do I need to do to "knock the ball out of the park"?	I have delivered x and I am eager to make a greater impact. Based on your expertise and knowledge of my background, any advice?
Organizational Savvy	What does it take to be successful here? Do you think I have what it takes?	What do I need to know about the culture? How are decisions made?	I am curious, what can you tell me about the people who have moved successfully from x to y?
Value to business	What skills do I need to develop?	I would like your feedback. Where do you think I can make the biggest impact?	I understand that our organization is moving in x direction and I see three possible ways to contribute. What is your perspective on the future direction of the business?

Issue	Mentor	Advisor	Advocate
Visibility	I will follow up on your suggestions and meet with X.	Who do you recommend that I meet in order to have a better understanding of this issue?	Thank you for the opportunity to present at x…

Who are your mentors, advisors, and advocates? Are you cultivating these important relationships and benefitting from them? Ask yourself these questions.

Answer the following questions and take the appropriate actions:

	Questions	Yes/No	Actions
ALERT?	▪ Do I have 3 to 5 mentors, each of whom contributes uniquely (admire, inspire, inform, teach, guide, etc.)? ▪ Does my manager provide valuable guidance and developmental opportunities? ▪ Is my "circle" well rounded and complete? If not, what viewpoints is it missing? ▪ Given the decision process regarding my next opportunity, have I developed one to three solid advocates?		
ADJUST?	▪ Am I informed and knowledgeable about potential mentor, advisors or advocates? ▪ Have I developed and practiced several succinct ways to convey who I am, what I want and how they can help?		
ALIGN?	▪ Do I keep my mentors, advisors and advocates in the loop? ▪ Do I follow up appropriately to build/ extend the relationship?		
ACT?	▪ Do I know how to maximize my time with my mentors? ▪ Do I let advisors know in advance the purpose of the meeting: advice, decision, brainstorm, get motivated? ▪ Do I show that I am gracious and appreciative of the time they spend?		

5

How Can I Anticipate and Embrace Change?

The purpose of life is to live it, to taste experience to the utmost,
to reach out eagerly and without fear for newer and richer
experience.

— Eleanor Roosevelt —

Paul rose through the operations side of the firm, his reputation secured through astute leadership of the company's largest plants. After successfully turning around a site in the Midwest, Paul accepted a corporate position at headquarters.

> My head was spinning! In two weeks, I went from managing 800 people, with clear lines of control and very defined goals and deliverables, to a role with zero direct reports and what felt like very squishy KPIs. All my previous promotions had been "more, more, more." More people, more plants, more products. This one was "new, new, new." New role, new skills, new everything. In my old job I was in charge. Now I'm standing in line—"Take a number!"

Paul could laugh about it, but his assessment was right on. He was experiencing a change that takes many executives by surprise—the change from a role with authority to one based on influence. The skills that got Paul there—sharp analysis, hard-nosed negotiations, a laser focus on the bottom line—were just the price of admission. They weren't the ones that could keep him there. To survive, Paul had to change; to succeed, Paul had to get out in front of change.

What does this change mean?

The differences between a *role* change and an *organizational* change are qualitative, not quantitative. Like Paul, you have moved up organizationally because your superiors recognize your skills and capacities, and they reward you with more responsibility. Then one day, you are offered an opportunity that demands something you have not—indeed, could not have—demonstrated yet. You now have to consider what it takes to "get there" in this new role. You will have to develop a new capacity and adjust to the changes you now confront. It may feel like opening a door to a room you didn't even know was there; that is how Paul felt.

> Nothing was written down. It was clandestine knowledge and I was expected to lead a team that didn't report to me. We always had defined processes in place in my old job. I had to change my habits. This may sound simplistic but instead of taking notes I started asking questions.

This situation will test your agility and require quick and clever understanding. You need to be nimble to see what is on the horizon, stay up-to-date, and embrace changes. Because whether it's a new professional role, organizational change, product or process innovation, the birth of a child or her departure for college, change is one constant you can rely on—and its intensity and pace only increase as you move up. You can't prevent change, even if you are happy with things as they are. You can resist it—and be run over by it—or you can be open to it, catch the wind in your sails and use it to reach your goals.

If your manager and colleagues didn't see you as being open to new ideas and willing to adapt your behavior and move in new directions, you would not have attained your current level of success. You have demonstrated an ability to notice emerging trends and lead your organization to meet them. And you are probably the first to embrace a new technology or share a new restaurant with your friends, who are out-of-the-box thinkers like you. So, if agility is already a strength, why are we focusing on being open to change? Because not all changes are of your own design or choosing, nor are they on your schedule or at your convenience. Because the higher you climb, the more important it is to stay open to change and be willing to change yourself, and to do this you must be open to new experiences in all areas of your life. It is easy for success to lead to complacency and for comfortable routines to become ruts. To avoid falling into a rut, you need to work on your professional agility just as an athlete works on physical agility. You can start by understanding how you relate to change.

Do you want to change or stay in your rut?

How do you respond to change? Do you avoid it, or do you say "Bring it on!"? Do you see change as a continual flow or as episodic and event-driven? When you face change that originates outside your control, are you worried? afraid? excited? What do you need to know before you can embrace a change? The answers to these questions depend largely on whether you perceive the change as an opportunity or a threat, because your brain reacts differently to each. If your brain sees the change as positive it releases dopamine, causing a feeling of pleasure. But the neural reaction to "danger" triggers panic. You actually *think less*. Everyone's threshold and definition of "dangerous" change is different—some people love roller coasters, some hate them. What kinds of change signal "danger" to you?

When you know how you typically relate to change, you can anticipate your reaction and prepare yourself to move forward. Some people respond to change with analysis. They want to understand the details, the rationale, the possible outcomes good and bad; once they get their answers, they can move forward. Others respond more emotionally; new situations temporarily lower their confidence and belief in their abilities, so they need to remind themselves of past successes and consider how they will handle the challenge.

Anne knew that she was in a rut:

> I call myself a middling "C" performer although my performance rating is consistently a "B." I know that I am behind the learning curve when it comes to the sophisticated products we now sell. With the coming reorganization, I will no longer make calls with a specialist. I will be on my own and there will be no place for me to hide. I don't have the confidence.

To help your brain see "opportunity" when faced with a big change, focus on *choice*, not on *change*. Given where you want to go and what you want to achieve, what choices can you make that will help you reach your goals? Anne realized that her success was in her hands. She could choose to learn the new products instead of waiting to be "found out" and risk losing her job.

To identify your options, you must assess which way the wind is blowing. Just as in golf, tennis, sailing, or running, having the wind at your back will propel you forward. Check the wind direction from the vantage point of your new position—has it changed? Which sail will you raise, which club will you select? How much spin will you put on the ball? Agility will help you go with the flow, even harness the change.

A technology shift led my client Rajiv's organization to a corporate restructuring and a new value proposition. The CEO identified Rajiv to lead the division into a new market—a totally different role for him. "Great news, *but* …." the hugely increased visibility of Rajiv's new role made him question his ability to succeed. Although he felt ready for the change, he knew he would have to work in entirely new ways and navigate a new structure.

> This is a serious promotion. I will be reporting directly to the CEO. I am mentally ready to be in charge of a lot of people, even though that's new for me. But things have changed. All the things that became routines over the last five years fell like dominos in three days. It will be a tough transition and I am under the microscope.

Rajiv knew that he would have to gain new, different skills on the fly. It would be a big challenge, with no guarantee of success.

What if you aren't sure you like this change?

We won't waste time talking about resisting a change you disagree with. You are experienced and senior enough to know that you will lend your support to ensure success for the team and the organization. Unless the proposal is actually unethical, your choice is to get on board with the change, or on board the next train outa' Dodge! Passive resistance doesn't work, and if you "go along to get along" it won't take long for your boss and peers to notice your sleepwalking.

A much better approach is to discover how this change will be beneficial or valuable to you. "W.I.I.F.M." (What's In It For Me?) isn't about being selfish—it's about committing yourself to the change, finding the win-win. When you see the benefit you can communicate the change in a positive and compelling way to your employees, clients, and stakeholders who will be able to sense that you too are with the program.

Even when you can see the benefits, something about the change may be bothering you. Don't get hung up on discussing how long change takes and how hard it is. These conversations become self-fulfilling

---

C-Suite Mindset

BE PERSISTENT AND SEIZE OPPORTUNITIES

Advisor: Mary Jo Meisner
Vice President for Communications, Community Relations
and Public Affairs, The Boston Foundation

I was a really good writer and that got me tapped to be a reporter for the *Philadelphia Daily News*. It was a rip-roaring newsroom and you had to be fast and unflappable; I quickly gained confidence as a reporter. I was confident doing the job I was doing when I got tapped to be a manager.

I didn't realize that I had the skills in me to be a manager and it was trial by fire: either you make it or you don't. I wondered: Am I able to handle breaking news and big stories? Will I survive the crucible of those things? You don't dwell on it, you rise to the occasion. You have to be persistent. In the news business, every day you have to put the paper up: it is a daily miracle. That's what they say and you realize how much you can get done if you keep pushing. Those experiences really form you if you pay attention and learn. You can turn anything into your own opportunity. Be opportunistic.

---

prophecies and they are fundamentally incorrect. In reality, people *can* and *do* change in an instant when confronted with the necessity or the right opportunity.

Instead of indulging in negative thinking or talking, I help my clients zero in on the root of their concern by drawing their attention to a model developed by my first organizational behavior professors, Lee Bolman and Terry Deal. Their work identifies the unavoidable downsides of organizational change. Even when the overall outcome is positive, it's important to recognize and acknowledge Bolman and Deals' four outcomes of change:

1 Change impacts individuals' need to feel effective, valued, and in control

2 Change will require new kinds of structural alignments

3 Change will cause conflict among those who will benefit and those who will not

4 Change will result in a loss of meaning for some members of the organization.

So don't be surprised if a change—even a "good" one—has you on edge! Consider these four outcomes of change and be clear about their effect on you, your colleagues and your organization. Pay attention to the impact on your self-esteem, confidence and your ability to feel competent. Don't let your doubts "close you down." Instead, address your concerns:

- If your self-esteem is under attack, focus on the qualities that led management to pick you for the new assignment.
- If your confidence is slipping, stop looking at your glass as half empty. Focus on the half-full glass: leverage your strengths and the lessons and best practices you have learned. Most important, project a positive, can-do attitude.
- If you lack a necessary competence, hire the right talent; rely on your team or build a stronger team so you can focus on providing strategic leadership for the group.

In sum, clear away your concerns and you will find that there is an opening for new experiences.

When Rajiv was offered a new position that demanded that he develop new skills, he took a moment to focus on his strengths, building his confidence for the work ahead.

> As different as this new role is for me, I can see why I was tapped for it. I am sure I can get this team heading in a new direction. As soon as I realized that this was going to happen I went into high gear to get things done. I did a lot of work on "who's who in the zoo." I took everyone and their spouses to a leadership retreat. I met 1:1 with my people on the West Coast, who had been feeling isolated.
>
> The interesting thing I noticed is that 40% of the people in the room were in new jobs; 20% hadn't been in leadership before. And I found that every one of my reports was deployed on a relatively small set of programs. I reorganized the whole team and redirected it to make things happen. I shared the vision with them and discovered that the group is very cohesive with a lot of camaraderie. I now feel that we can get out in front of this reorganization.

C-Suite Mindset

INVEST IN THE PEOPLE AROUND YOU

Advisor: Mike Ullman
CEO JCPenney, Macy's

JCPenney was a hundred-year-old company looking at the world through the rear mirror. I focused on renewing the culture. As CEO I wanted to personally know JCPenney, so I met with 30 people each month in a three-day class where we did table work on three topics; no lecturing—only conversations. Everybody had been a store manager and the biggest issue was restoring trust. Trust is the most important factor in being engaged. Before me, the culture had ensured no one ever admitted a mistake because they were in a race—they were hiding behind the numbers. I had a disagreement with one department head because he wanted to give everyone the same bonus. I asked, "Why do you think that that is fair? What if I think that it's fair for only one person—the person in the middle? And, by the way, you are paying them as if they were winning when they're not."

Are you ready for the next big change?

Picture the final match of the U.S. Open. Roger Federer waits to receive Raphael Nadal's serve. Perfectly balanced over slightly bent knees, relaxed yet totally alert, he is ready to move in any direction to meet the ball. As the ball leaves the racquet he anticipates its landing spot and gets there first. He is agile and ready. He knows his own strengths and weaknesses.

You can be equally ready to return any serve that comes your way, if you find your balance and anticipate future developments. In fact, when you develop your agility you'll actually enjoy responding to new challenges.

So take time now to prepare. What is the next change coming at you? How will you respond to it? Add your thoughts and ideas on the following page:

	Questions	Yes/No	Actions
ALERT?	<ul><li>Am I aware of the external factors affecting my industry/profession?</li><li>Do I have my ear to the "grapevine"?</li><li>Are my skills, knowledge, and competencies up to date?</li></ul>		
ADJUST?	<ul><li>Am I in a role or position that has a future?</li><li>Have I discussed with my manager the steps that I have taken to fill or close gaps?</li><li>Have I made a choice to make this change work for me?</li></ul>		
ALIGN?	<ul><li>Do I understand the benefit of this change to my organization, to my function/department and to the bottom line?</li><li>Do I understand how my role and responsibilities align in the new order of things?</li></ul>		
ACT?	<ul><li>Do I have a strategy to respond to this change?</li><li>Do I have the resources and support to successfully navigate this change?</li></ul>		

6

How Can I Meet the Challenge of Being the Only One Like Me?

The privilege of a lifetime is being who you are.
— Joseph Campbell —

Early in my career, having worked in the public sector and spent a year as a White House Fellow, I stepped into the corporate arena. My talents and capacities were recognized and rewarded by rapid advancement. Nonetheless, I was new to business and often felt like a "stranger in a strange land," so when I was promoted to director and invited to eat in the executive dining room, I had no idea of the magnitude of my accomplishment. Intellectually, I was up the task but politically—I had no clue how things worked.

In the 80s, there wasn't a formal women's or black network. The idea of social networks wasn't in the common business vocabulary as it is today—at most, people talked about "cliques." As one of the first black women to attain the level of director, I had no one to guide me, and no one reached out to help. As a result, after sitting uncomfortably in a sea of white men in the dining room, I gravitated back to eating lunch at my desk, completely unaware of the corporate faux pas I was committing. The honor of dining as an executive conveys status and provides the opportunity to expand relationships across business lines. But I literally left that opportunity "on the table" because I felt different from the others in the room.

Are you the only person like you in your organization?

We've come a long way since the 80s, and nowadays my awkward experience in the executive dining room is the exception instead of the norm. Recognizing the risk to their human resource investment, many companies take a proactive approach to the isolation I felt. For example in companies such as CITI that have active affinity groups, when a woman, black, Hispanic, or other non-dominant–group member is promoted to a position with access to the executive dining room, members of that group who already have that perk reach out and schedule the first few luncheons. The new person is welcomed and dines at a diverse table, not just with members of his or her apparent affinity group. The result is that new executives look like they belong and they are recognized as peers.

But many who view themselves as "the only one" are still eating alone at their desks today—perhaps you are reading this chapter over a sandwich yourself! If you feel isolated in your organization, you may believe that your advancement is limited by differences that set you apart from the predominant group. Even though that characteristic is only one part of your multi-faceted identity, it seems to define and limit you. What is the quality that makes you feel like the "only one"? Common answers include race, gender or sexual orientation. But people who come from different cultures also feel isolated: they have a different worldview, or they hesitate to speak up because English is their second language and they lack the "correct" words. Or you may think that you are "the only one" because you are hiding your struggles with Asperger's disorder, dyslexia, or a chronic disease, or you are married to an alcoholic, or you don't want others to know you have overcome a speech impediment. Given the variety of qualities or characteristics that can at times make people feel like outsiders, you can appreciate that many people face this challenge.

What is going on here?

First, be assured that you are not imagining your "outsider" status; you are not paranoid or overly sensitive. In fact, anyone who doesn't fit comfortably into the mold of whatever group predominates in the environment will feel "different" because groups naturally sort themselves along lines of similarity. Social scientists have documented how homogeneous groups identify "outsiders" based on relative distinctiveness, regardless of the special characteristic—for a relatively harmless example, witness the way tourists "stick out" from locals. There are several psychological theories as to why human beings define groups in this way, but we aren't going to discuss the causes or even decry this reality. Your job is to find a path to success in spite of your differences.

Noted management theorist Rosabeth Moss Kanter sums up the challenges facing members of any minority group in an organization composed mainly of majority individuals in her book, *A Tale of "O": On Being Different in an Organization.* Even in organizations with the best intentions and surrounded by well-meaning and educated colleagues, people who stand out for one reason or another have special hurdles to overcome. Except for certain unusual and extremely talented exceptions, "outsiders" just don't have the same opportunities to succeed for a number of reasons. First, there are the stereotypes: they "fear success" or "compete too aggressively," or they are only good at certain traditional roles. They may carry the extra burden of being seen as "test cases" (sometimes even publicly identified as such) and subject to extra scrutiny. They are held out as examples (good or bad) of their group, and called upon to "represent" their group's views as if all black/female/wheelchair-bound people thought the same. It is frustrating to be viewed through a lens that magnifies what is, after all, just one part of your total identity. No wonder many people in this situation choose one of these responses as a coping method and possible path to success:

- Overachievement—doing twice as much and being twice as good as members of the dominant group
- Blending in—trying to appear just like everyone else, essentially denying their own special characteristics
- Stepping out of the spotlight (and the competition)—taking a role behind the scenes or succeeding in safe and traditional areas

Are you working harder than everyone else, but it's not paying off?

Let's look at the temptation to overachieve. Many people believe that they have to work twice as hard as anyone else in order to be recognized and promoted over members of the dominant group. There can even be an "I'll show them" attitude driving their overachievement. But overachieving can backfire. Here's what happened to Tony:

> I always thought that my boss would be fair and when the time came all my hard work would pay off. I get in at 8:30AM and I don't leave until 9:00 p.m. I come in at least one day on the weekends. They all know that I do and frankly, it's the only way the work gets done. I know that my boss appreciates it.
>
> Now I see one guy is losing his job and the other is being promoted and I really thought that I would get that job because I have been doing a component of it functionally. I have never been the one to push but I am really hurt that he didn't give it to me.

You might think that quietly putting in long hours, working under the radar and not complaining would be the characteristics of a solid professional, but these practices have both positive and negative outcomes. The benefits are obvious—you develop a reputation for being a dependable and detail-oriented person who will get the job done. Your boss values you because in a pinch she can give you a tricky assignment and you will move heaven and earth and deliver with no complaints.

But here's the downside: as I always advise, you should look at *every* assignment carefully. When you take on an extra task without considering in advance how this project will provide either increased visibility or allow you to deepen or expand your professional experience, then you have wasted a big opportunity. If you accept extra work as "no big deal," without asking to have anything taken off your plate, you risk sabotaging your own efforts by shortchanging other work. Remember; as you move into senior levels you can't expect your hard work to automatically pay off. It's up to you to approach the challenge strategically and seek out opportunities that will showcase your abilities and/or prepare you for the next level. Remember to reach out to your "board of directors" for guidance. And take advantage of the strong relationship you have forged with your boss by your hard work to date.

Just working hard doesn't guarantee that you will reap the benefits. To ensure that you do, first define for yourself your next two career steps. Then pursue the experiences or projects that will give you the skills and/or visibility you need to meet your goal. Learn the culture and language of your future opportunity—who do you need to meet to gain a better understanding of the future role, or who can you collaborate with to bolster your business? Then, leverage your relationship with your boss to move to your next opportunity.

Do you feel like you have to stop being yourself to succeed?

When your cultural norms are different from the mainstream, or your upbringing hasn't prepared you to march in step with the dominant group, it may seem that your choices are limited: either blend in or step out. With strong cultural traditions of your own, you may feel you can't or don't want to emulate the majority. But it is possible to hold on to the best of yourself while succeeding.

My client Mercedes was viewed as hard working but shy. Her cultural background did not prepare her to feel comfortable contradicting her manager—she hadn't learned how to be assertive without feeling or appearing aggressive. Her manager knew that Mercedes wanted to succeed and recommended her for a leadership development program sponsored by the firm's diversity council. In addition to classroom instruction with personal assessment and individual coaching, this program included a unique interface with senior management: over breakfast or lunch, senior leaders shared their stories of how they arrived in their positions and what they learned along the way.

> These sessions really opened my eyes. As I got to know the senior leaders, I discovered that while they share a set of consistent values, they employ very different leadership styles. Through the coaching, I was able to role-play different ways to respond to situations until I developed a style that worked and felt authentic to me.

The program culminated with members making presentations to senior leaders. The previously "shy" Mercedes showed herself to be decidedly confident. From the perspective of senior management she now had the "right mix" of leadership behaviors and she was soon offered a lateral move that gave her more visibly and responsibility, putting her on the track for promotion.

Mercedes learned that it is not necessary to abandon your own culture or "blend in" to succeed. There are many successful leadership styles, and you can discover one that will work for you. It may help to ask successful people who are "like you" how they "made it." The important thing is to find ways to display your abilities.

> We are all different from one another,
> but in the important things we are all alike.
> *W. Edwards Deming*

Handle your preferences for styles of dress, levels of formality, and other more visible manifestations of cultural differences with sensitivity. You don't need to abandon your own practices, but don't over display your differentness either. Be sure your dress, carriage, and voice make it clear you are ready to do business. After all, you want the conversation to be about your competence, not your culture.

Are you playing by a different set of rules?

The myth of getting to the top promises that if you work hard and keep your nose clean you will be recognized and promoted on your merit.

That's great advice when you begin your career and your competency, credibility and results are on display. That is, when you are making your mark. To reach higher levels, people outside the mainstream often hold fast to the ideal of the meritocracy, while watching their peers draw on other tools in addition to their functional skills. Closer to the top of the organizational pyramid, functional prowess is assumed and new factors come into play. In a competitive field in which everyone is competent, characteristics such as organizational savvy and "fit" come to the fore. If you cling to expectations of a strict meritocracy, you will be disappointed.

For example, Rashi expected that excellent performance in his job would assure his promotion. Like many individuals who receive their education outside the United States, he had faced a more rigorous and unforgiving education process, defined by an inflexible curriculum and competitive examinations. The system is hierarchical and formulaic: follow the rules, do the work and achieve success. Cultures with these ranked educational systems are more likely to value fitting in versus speaking up and standing out. But, as Rashi learned, promotion at senior levels depends on much more than success within the boundaries of a job description.

> I always worked hard and thought nothing of it. In India you get one chance and if you don't score high you have no future. Based on my grades, I got accepted to one of the best engineering schools and my future was secured. I work hard here, too, and was promoted early to director. I've always exceeded all my performance metrics. I don't ask for anything; I don't want to draw attention to myself. I do my job. Lately, my boss has been asking me to speak up more; she wants me to go on more customer visits. I don't know ... I'm more comfortable on the engineering side, and that's where my job is focused.

Rashi's current position is on the engineering side of the business, but his future—if he has one in this organization—depends on his manager and other senior people seeing him in a new way, as a savvy leader who understand the business as a whole and is ready to contribute in different ways to its success.

If this is your situation, apply the same discipline, ability to adapt, and multi-cultural outlook you used to get hired to successfully manage your career now. Focus your academic prowess on this new curriculum, only this time it's up to you—not your teachers or boss—to design the curriculum and determine your success. Your first task is to expand your understanding and appreciation of the business. Learn the language of business—the culture. Who gets ahead? Why? What makes them successful? Understand the rituals: meeting for drinks, socializing and networking. Especially important for people from cultures that discourage self-promotion, eliminate artificial barriers: an "open door policy" means that the door is open to *you*.

Are you hiding something important about yourself?

If you didn't grow up in the country club set where professional and personal lives are blurred, you may still be operating by the old adage of "I keep my business and personal lives separate." This is a failed strategy that many women, LGBT, and people of color employ. The divide begins early: "We don't want those people to see how we live. They think they are better than us." Or, "I work all day; I don't want to have to work all night being around them." Or maybe you were just taught to keep your personal life personal. From Haiti and the first in her family to make it, Bea took pride in being direct and, while at work, *working*.

> I am not really a people person. With clients you have to make small talk but for the most part chit-chatting is a waste of time. I honestly don't understand why people do it. They look at me like I have three heads.

The explanation for Bea's behavior can be found in Malcolm Gladwell's book *Outliers*:

> Practical intelligence, the savvy to know what to say to whom, doesn't come easily to poorer children. Children who grow up in poverty are more submissive when addressing adults and authority figures. They aren't raised to assert themselves. This disadvantage can result in a lifelong struggle with interpersonal communications.

Keeping personal life personal can be especially difficult if you are the success story in your family or if have a challenges at home—responsibility for a sick or aging parent, a wife with Lou Gehrig's disease, a husband who is unemployed, or children with special issues. Perhaps you cope daily with a medical condition or mental illness, or you struggle with the crises and shame caused by a family member's substance abuse or legal

---

C-Suite Mindset

IT'S NOT PERSONAL

Advisor: Colette Philips
President and CEO, CPC Communications

When I came to the Boston from Antigua, my friends tried to protect me by warning me that Boston was no place for a black woman to start a business. I believed in myself and followed my heart. I started out in a nonprofit and after working diligently I discovered that my boss had not only hired another person at my level, she was paying him seven thousand dollars more than I was making. I was so angry—I thought it was racist—I wrote her a scathing letter. Lucky for me, before pressing "send" I talked it over with a close friend who knew how organizations operated. She told me, "Never put things in writing. Sit down with her. What you put in writing goes into your file. When you act out of anger, you say and do things that you can never take back and you act irrationally."

I have learned to let my email sit in my draft folder, without putting the person's name in the send box, because you can't take it back. Getting there is recognizing you can't personalize any situation. Don't take everything personally—it is usually not about you.

I also surround myself with people who believe and have faith in me—faith in my ability to conquer whatever barriers and faith that when the wolves come to the door I will survive. I am blessed by having cheerleaders and gentle critics.

---

problems. Or you may believe you must keep your sexual persuasion a secret. Few things cause more feelings of isolation than trying to hide something about yourself. As we discuss in Chapter 7, don't imagine that you can wall off an important part of your life. On the contrary, you can be certain that even if your boss or colleagues don't know exactly *what* is wrong, they will know *something* is wrong. Most people are unconsciously sensitive to the cues that others are "hiding" something, and as a result they trust those people less. Ultimately, you will feel even more isolated! You may even find yourself dealing with untrue rumors as your colleagues try to fill in the gaps in your story. Or you may just isolate yourself more.

> I told my boss that my mom has cancer, but I am not going to tell my colleagues because I don't want them to think that I am not doing my part. But my colleagues keep asking me if I am OK and this has become very annoying. They keep prying. I have stopped going out to lunch with them because I don't want to talk about it—they don't need to know. I am a private person.

The solution for this kind of isolation is to talk, in a limited way that you define and control, to a select group of people. As risky as this may seem, it is much better for your manager and colleagues to understand that you are dealing with issues at home than for them to think you are dissatisfied in your position or don't like your team.

How can you succeed and still be true to yourself?

Many companies have taken a proactive approach to meet these challenges of "outsiders" in the organization—and it's about time, given that the United States will be "majority minority" in just a few decades! But if your company hasn't recognized this issue and undertaken to address it, you can still take steps on your own to deal with the challenge of your difference. Take the initiative yourself. Here are some things you must do:

1 Seek input and advice from others. Find a mentor or sponsor to teach you the ropes. Look for people "like you" and ask them what they did to be successful. Talk to others in your group; support one another and share coping strategies. Get to know members of the mainstream group and use them as resources too—they have valuable expertise. In short, find your "tribe" and connect with people who inspire you, not just the ones who look or think like you. By reaching across group boundaries to join different networks, you enrich everyone.

2 Recognize and understand the special burdens of being in the "other" group. Being aware of how groups identify and stereotype "others" will help you decide how to manage your experience. Recognize that you will be expected to serve as a model or example of your group; preserve your energy for your job and avoid overload from too much service as a spokesperson.

Develop your diplomatic skills so you can handle the inevitable awkward situations, but don't get riled up by every comment or joke, especially if offense is not intended.

3 Relate as an individual. Develop relationships with people in the mainstream group as individuals, rather than seeing them as a monolithic group. Do what you want others to do: focus on common ground, not on differences that set you apart.

4 Develop the skills required to succeed. Be sure your competence, credibility and communication abilities are not in question; make sure people talk about your abilities, not your differences. Find ways to develop your competencies, not just take on more work. Learn the rules—always have your elevator speech ready—and understand how the game is played.

5 Identify and leverage the value of your "outsider" perspective. You have a unique perspective if you grew up in another country and especially if you are multi-lingual and well traveled. If raised in the United States, your economic and cultural perspective can provide real world demographic insights. Cultivate your experiences and be a voice for often overlooked or underserved niches in the marketplace.

On the following page, answer the questions and take the actions appropriate to your unique situation:

	Questions	Yes/No	Actions
ALERT?	• What is the unique characteristic that makes me the only one? • Does that unique characteristic separate me from the mainstream? • Am I acting in a manner that "separates" me from the mainstream? • What is the value I bring to my organization?		
ADJUST?	• Do I understand the culture? • Am I able to describe the variety of styles, approaches or behavior that lead to success? • Do I know what I need to do—for example, how I need to communicate to succeed?		
ALIGN?	• Am I connected to the mainstream norms, values and behavior of my organization? • Do I have mentors; advisors and advocates who help me navigate the organizational culture? • Do I follow up appropriately to build and extend my relationships?		
ACT?	• Am I actively and appropriately involved? • Have I avoided being sidelined, overachieving or trying to fit in? • Am I open to new approaches and new experiences? • Am I able to be authentic in my organization?		

7

How Can I Deal
with Stress or Failure?

The bamboo that bends is stronger
than the oak that resists.
— Japanese proverb —

When asked how she copes with stress, "Madame Secretary" Madeleine Albright replied to the audience at the Commonwealth Institute: "Isn't it obvious? I eat!" The audience chuckled along with her. Her authenticity, her quickness in telling the truth about herself resonated with everyone in the room. I felt that she was speaking directly to me: I, too, eat when stressed. In fact, some years ago I gained twenty pounds as my marriage dissolved in divorce. My physical appearance has always been core to my personal brand; after all I had been a body builder and a New England Patriots Cheerleader. Friends come to me for advice on diet and exercise. The stress and the embarrassing twenty pounds actually caused a dramatic shift in my personality, transforming me from an active extrovert into a reclusive couch potato. Stress can do that to you.

What is your physical response to stress?

You may think you can "handle it," but your body responds to all stress, both physical and emotional. Hormonal secretions—the same ones that trigger the "fight or flight" response in animals facing predators—occur even when you do not consciously acknowledge the stress you are under. As your body focuses on the problem causing the stress, your digestive, sexual, and immune systems are diverted from less critical tasks of daily life and comfort, often with unpleasant consequences.

Nowadays we have a wider range of responses to stress than simply fighting or fleeing. You might argue or get angry, or, like me, you might withdraw to cookies and the couch. Your response will naturally vary depending on the circumstances. The important thing is to recognize when you are under stress and take note of your response.

I have a very talented client who actually continued to gain weight after we discussed the fact that he was overweight and that his appearance might derail his career. Richard explained his weight gain this way:

> My boss keeps telling me to slow down, but I am now responsible for managing the flow of all people in the region. My schedule is crazy, so I eat—lunch with clients, snack from the vending machine in the evening, and eat dinner around 10 p.m.

What is the "believable" explanation you give for your behavior?

It's easy to make excuses for your behavior without acknowledging the stress you are under. Recently promoted, Richard was hell bent on not failing—fear of failure is very stressful. If you are overweight don't dismiss it by saying that it is the inevitable outcome of business-related socializing. Notice that your colleagues are making a different choice than the one you are making: they are not overeating, over-drinking or engaged in non-thinking behavior associated with stress. They are being mindful and present. When Richard focused on his situation, he saw it differently:

> It is getting more stressful. I have less time to think. I am swamped. I don't have a chance to focus—I have no time to focus. We have 10 analysts coming from Singapore, London and Australia and I am in the process of allocating the 1:1 time for my group. However, my time management is not so good. I tend to jump around to different tasks. I used to devote the afternoon to administrative tasks and use the morning to work with clients. I was actually disciplined. With the pressure that I am under I don't have the time.

A zebra facing a marauding lion has no behavioral choices—instinct takes over. Modern people can make choices, but we can only make the right choices when we are mindful and present to three realities:

1 Our mood
2 The conditions of stress
3 Our habitual response to stress

Once conscious of my mood and the situation, and aware of my habitual stress-related behavior, e.g., eat cookies number one, two and three—I can literally wake myself up from the stress-induced fog and observe the consequences of my action. Sometimes I will say aloud, "What are you doing? What else can you do now that will make you feel good?" I remember that I can choose a different path.

The American Psychological Association (APA) reports that the causes of stress in America are as follows:

1 Money (75 percent)
2 Work (70 percent)
3 The economy (67 percent)
4 Relationships (58 percent)
5 Family responsibilities (57 percent)
6 Family health problems (53 percent)
7 Personal health concerns (53 percent)
8 Job stability (49 percent)
9 Housing costs (49 percent) and
10 Personal safety (32 percent)

It isn't surprising that money and work are causes of stress and that stress often leads to disruptive and destructive behavior. Here is an example from the press: "Richard Parkes" (a pseudonym adopted by the writer) had it all—a beautiful wife, two gorgeous children and a flourishing media career. So why did he embark on an affair that would rip his life apart forever? Stress.

> Subconsciously I'd been looking for a pick-me-up after the follow-up project had been disappointing and a third had no takers. I still got some freelance production work but I felt the pizzazz in my working life had gone.

The APA also reports that although most adults realize that stress can adversely affect a person's health, people don't think that it will affect *their* health. Stress creates a major *blind spot*. Remember that, by definition, a blind spot is something that you don't see (we'll learn more about blind spots in Chapter 11). However, it is important to recognize that *others* are noticing your stress. For example, Julia had just moved from the East Coast to Texas to manage a geographically dispersed team; her boss and senior leadership team were 1300 miles and a time zone away at corporate headquarters. A senior engineer responsible for the launch of a global product, she told me:

> I am stressed in a couple of areas on most days. I have to continue to develop relationships with my people; figure out how to man-

age long distance and in a distributed area; learn more about the financials that drive the business and establish relationships with the customer base—who they are and what they want. With the differences in time zones it makes for a very long day.

When I collected the 360-degree feedback from her colleagues and manager they said:

> Julia seems to have changed. She used to be so friendly and open and now she is a "loner." She will sit in an off-site meeting for two days and not talk. I wonder, who are her followers and who will take a bullet for her? She has her head down and hasn't shared her vision. We want the old Julia back.

Julia was being noticed for all the wrong reasons. She wanted to get back to her old self and be the "superstar" that earned the promotion. However, she made the mistake that "superstars" often do: she worked harder and longer, submerging herself in her work, until she was a "loner" with nothing to say.

We have been talking so far about stress that might be seen as a positive—the stress that comes from being recognized as a contributor and being handed more work to deliver. But another source of stress is failure, and its results can be even more dangerous than the stress of success.

How is your behavior or personality changing?

Many of my clients initially try to convince me that they can compartmentalize their lives, but I haven't seen anyone successfully do so. Compartmentalizing means that you put your life into separate buckets or silos. The goal is to "hide" a part of who you are. From my work at the FBI at the dawn of the behavioral science unit (now popularized as CSI) I know that serial killers such as Charles Bundy are able to "hide" who they really are. However, the average person is rarely successful.

Why? People who try to "withhold information" appear to be keeping a secret and most of us have a "nose" for sniffing out secrets. We sense a change in mood, we may see behavior that doesn't "fit" and in some instances we get the feeling that something is going on and there is "an elephant in the room." Here is a glaring example that something was going on:

> Rene-Thierry Magon de la Villehuchet's wife called their Connecticut yacht club on Monday to cancel their $2,500-a-year membership, a staffer said.

"She was crying," said Milford Yacht Club treasurer John DePalma, whose secretary took Claudine Villehuchet's call on Monday. "She said she loved the club and she said she hated to drop out, but she had to for personal reasons. She didn't give any indication."

Villehuchet's wife was caught up in stress. Her personal life was a key component of her husband's professional life, where the country club isn't a perk; it is place where deals get made and relationships deepened.

Rene-Thierry Magon de la Villehuchet, 65, the founder and chief executive officer of an investment fund that lost millions it had invested in Bernard L. Madoff Investment Securities, was found dead at 7:50 this morning at his Access International Advisors office in Manhattan.

He had been trying to recover the money that Access International raised in Europe and invested through Mr. Madoff's business, according to La Tribune, which first reported the news, citing an unnamed source.

The couple tried to hide the disaster but it all came crashing down in public humiliation and family tragedy: Bottom line: don't let the pressure build by "keeping secrets." It is up to you to raise your concerns, issues and challenges. And, it's up to you to decide how much you want to disclose. Don't keep the lid on by thinking, "I don't want to tell them everything." Believe me when I tell you—"they" don't want or need to hear *everything*. Your boss and colleagues know you and realize that you are not only a private person but also a proud one. As a result, give them the headlines so that they understand why your behavior has changed. Don't create a problem for yourself by giving TMI [too much information]. By handling it in this way, you are managing your brand during a crisis—and your crisis is not destroying your brand. Always be proactive.

What is the "headline" that helps explain your mood or change in behavior?

Stress at home often spills over into the workplace. Your colleagues may not know exactly "what" is going on but they know that "something" has changed. Executives at all levels rarely have the skill to deal with stress-related personal problems and most resort to "I am not the type of person to share my personal problems at work." They insist, "I don't bring that to work" even though they walk around like a cartoon character with a bubble of doom over its head. I know; I tried to hide the stress I was under when my parents were no longer able to care for themselves and I had to play a key role in the decision to move them into a nursing home. My response to the stress: submerge myself in work. You would see me at the office at 10:00 at night, almost always the last person to leave the building.

What are you doing to avoid confronting your stressful concern(s)?

Here is another example, from the headlines. Claude Allen, Assistant for Domestic Policy under George W. Bush, was arrested in March 2006 for a series of alleged thefts in Montgomery County, Maryland. Allen admitted to committing refund theft by fraudulently returning shoplifted items in stores for cash. Police said he credited more than $5,000 to his credit card through dozens of transactions at several stores. By any measure Allen's behavior was bizarre. He didn't need the money—his annual salary as a White House advisor was $160,000. He pleaded guilty to theft and shed tears during his sentencing hearing, apologizing to his wife, family, and friends, saying, "I lost perspective and failed to restrain myself." Allen's wife cited White House job stress and family stress in raising four young children as reasons for her husband's shoplifting.

Stress creates a distortion. Stress can lead to disruptive and self-destructive behavior. Some cases can be dramatic and tragic especially when they involve public disgrace and failure. When a top HSBC banker was found hanged in the room of a five-star London hotel, *The Mail* quoted bank sources as saying, 'What happened came as a complete shock to management. Some were aware that he was undergoing personal problems but nothing like what was happening in reality." Police later revealed that a note found in the room "suggested problems in his marriage" were to blame.

You can't keep a lid on stress. It is like the pressure cooker that my mother would warn us kids to stay away from: "Be careful, the steam is going to escape—if it doesn't, that lid will come off and hurt you!"

Are you losing control?

I have noticed that stress and fear of failure are often linked especially for individuals with high standards or, as some might say, unrealistic expectations—of performance. Simply using the term "unrealistic expectations"

C-Suite Mindset

DON'T PUT A PILLOW OVER YOUR HEAD

Advisor: James "Chips" Stewart
Director of Public Safety for CNA's Safety and Security Team.
Retired Chief of Detectives Oakland Police Department, Oakland
California

I was scheduled to conduct an investigation when I got word that my mother passed away unexpectedly. My initial thought was to cancel but I got on the plane very tearful. I knew that my colleagues would say "Give him a break, he is not going to be at his best." However, I thought about the message St. Francis of Assisi delivered to his despondent disciples returning from Morocco: You have to be cheerful despite the circumstances.

When I think back over the years—if you are in a position of authority you have a professional responsibility to ensure that quality of product. You can't say, "I screwed up the budget because I had a bad day." We think that we need our secrets or failures quiet and hidden, but we need to share—we are not going to be destroyed by the situation. People who only depend on themselves eventually get done in. Remember Scrooge's response to Jacob Marley's warning: "These are the chains I forged in life"? Stay connected in the moment and don't be like Scrooge who put a pillow over his head.

is a tip-off that the person is not grounded in reality. Unfortunately, occupying a different reality can be isolating and often in that isolation the individual determines, well before his or her peers, "I am losing control and I am not going to make it." What I see and have personally experienced is that stress builds up over time and eventually the lid blows off—like the pressure cooker my mother warned us to stay away from.

Who will listen non-judgmentally while you vent?

I can give more examples of the secrets people keep that are the source of stress that eventually spills over into work: like the client taking care of spouse with ALS, or one dealing with fertility issues, or men and women who are "closeted" and are fearful about the upcoming retreat to which significant others are invited. In each case, the client has tried to keep a lid on his personal stressors and the reading from the boss and colleagues is "something is wrong here—it's affecting his work and our communications. It has to stop."

If you are under stress, don't push it to a failure. Approach your manager before your manager approaches you. Let her know about the personal issues at the source of your stress so that your behavior doesn't seem erratic or off-kilter. It is important to realize that you are not the first or the only person to be in this situation. You are *not* alone. It probably isn't your fault or the result of a personal failing. Lift the lid.

1 Tell a trusted friend how you feel.
2 When asked, "What is going on? What's wrong?" tell them.
3 Remember, you don't have to reveal everything but say enough so that the person can connect and appreciate your concern and especially why it might be showing up in your behavior.
4 Be kind to yourself. Don't view your concern as a "dirty little secret." You should remember that, as isolated as it may make you feel, you are really not the only one facing this.
5 Health issues must be addressed—confronting the consequences of stress can actually ease the stress itself. Work exercise into your life; you can at least find time to walk, or take stairs instead of the elevator.

If you talk about it, will your manager think you can't do your job?

Now, you may have read all of this and be thinking: I am not going to say that I am "stressed" because they will think that I can't do my job or that I am overwhelmed. I agree, choose your words carefully. If you have a great relationship with your boss, the kind in which you talk about everything openly, it's likely that you have found a way to talk about the ups and downs of your life and your boss and colleagues know about the stressors that have occurred in your life. For example, they know that when Jennifer was a preemie you slept in the hospital; they can understand that now that she is off to college stress at home is rising because you don't know how you will cope—or who you will be—with an "empty nest."

Remember, there is no formulaic answer. It's up to you to find the "right" words to convey your concerns so that you can make space to accommodate the emotions that accompany the stress. Find a positive and productive way to ease the pressure.

I think that you will be surprised to find that your manager is supportive, accepting, even sympathetic when you bring it up. Several of my clients found that their manager or colleagues offered strategies to deal with the issue, others found that by sharing their situation they developed a new level of trust and a deeper relationships. Almost all noticed a shift in their behavior after getting the situation off their chests. When you open a discussion in a closed area it's like opening a window to let the fresh air in. What are you waiting for?

Add your thoughts and ideas below to expand your repertoire of responses to stress.

	Questions	Possible Answers	Actions
ALERT?	What is the effect on my health or behavior?	▪ Can't sleep ▪ Can't concentrate ▪ Over eating ▪ Not eating ▪ Drinking ▪ Depressed	
ADJUST?	How is it affecting my work?	▪ Inconsistent ▪ Over-prepared/under-prepared ▪ Micro-managing ▪ Forgetful ▪ Feel pressured and swamped ▪ Overwhelmed ▪ Break in communications ▪ Distant ▪ Disruptive ▪ Inappropriate actions ▪ Unethical behavior	
ALIGN?	Who do I need to talk to?	▪ Friends ▪ Family ▪ Co-workers	
ACT?	What do I need to do to ease the pressure?	▪ Delegate ▪ Take time off ▪ See doctor	

8

Am I Getting the Maximum Benefit Out of My Situation?

Carpe Diem! Seize the day!

Hand picked by the president of his foundation for the senior development position, Howard is suddenly in a new and unfamiliar milieu.

> I was very successful as an individual player. I skipped two (maybe three) levels to take on the role because my marketing and outreach activity caught the president's attention. But now I'm weighed down by an organization of 25, with more positions open than filled. I need to deliver at the same "individual" level and now I've got these new leadership responsibilities too.

Howard has to learn to balance external outreach with administration and he is in danger of getting lost in the weeds. He is focusing on his new deliverables and has hardly given a thought to the more subtle aspects of his new role. Although he hasn't realized it, his promotion brings more than new responsibilities, a larger staff, and a bigger salary—it transports him to a new peer group and a seat at the decision table. Luckily, Howard now has several new tools at his disposal to address his new challenges; his success will depend on how skillfully he puts them to use. In fact, if he doesn't use these new tools, odds are he won't be successful in his new role *or* reach the next level.

Are you getting the maximum benefit out of your situation?

Congratulations on your new role. You are probably enthusiastic about your newfound opportunity and ready to prove yourself in the new position. This may be the first time you are the final decision maker or in a position with line responsibility. You may be accountable for a new product introduction, or your financial portfolio may include emerging markets. Whatever your new role, you are eager to get to work, produce results, meet deliverables and in the process show your manager that you are up for the task. Not so fast! Now is *not* the time to get down into the weeds. Now's the time to look up, across, and out and ask, "How can I maximize and leverage this opportunity to move up, or move on?"

per·qui·site /'pərkwəzit/

*Noun. A thing regarded as a special right or
privilege enjoyed as a result of one's position*

Tangible and intangible perquisites—perks—come with every new role as you advance in an organization. When you are just starting out, the perks of a promotion might include a more generous travel allowance or something as simple as a quiet cubicle. Have you identified the tangible and intangible perks that come with your new role? If you can't name them, this is your wake up call—it is time to look beyond the money and that long-awaited office with a window. It is time to leverage your situation for success.

Don't overlook the most important non-monetary perquisites that accompany your new role: access and influence. Whatever your level, a promotion always widens your circle of access and influence. That includes access to resources—people, time, and information—as well as the increased weight or influence that your words and ideas can convey. Do you remember the "Six Degrees of Separation" parlor game? Well, you've just moved one degree closer to resources you can marshal for success.

In his new role, Howard not only has the authority of his new position; he is also a member of the president's cabinet. Membership in the cabinet—his access—requires that he learn the implicit and explicit ways in which the members of the team interact. The informal or cultural expectations surrounding his role are at least as important as his formal responsibilities. After all, Howard wouldn't have the job if his management team didn't believe that he could handle the deliverables. He has to show that he is equally adept at his informal duties.

Howard has an untapped advantage in his role: his two-level promotion, engineered by the president, was a strong signal that Howard embodied the desired future leadership style. In fact, with the upcoming product launch, he has been the president's "right-hand" person. Yet Howard allowed himself to be dragged down into the weeds because he was unaware of the access and influence that came with his new job. He forgot to ask: what are the perks?

Are you taking advantage of the access your role provides?

It's not enough to just *have* access. In your new role, you have access to everyone in your new organizational function or scope. Sound intimidating? It can be at first, but remember: you are the new kid on the block and your co-workers are curious to get to know you. When you move into a new role, the organizational dynamics shift. New relationships form or old ones deepen based on the access that you now have. You may be surprised to find that people now want access to you!

Look around and up. In your new role, you have access to a wider circle —offering unique experiences, perspective and information.

- Your manager
- Your manager's manager. Why? Your manager's manager probably approved your new position and knows your background and strengths.
- Your HR generalist or manager
- Your immediate team members
- Colleagues in your department or within your organizational function
- Clients, customers, vendors
- Administrative staff/resources
- Janitorial or cleaning staff. Why? Working unobtrusively, they often hear and see things before they are formally announced
- Front desk personnel
- Competitors

Do you know how to use your access?

Having access and *using* access may be miles apart, and if you don't take advantage of your access it does you no good. You may *have* access to the people mentioned, but are you taking advantage of that access? Why not? The answers I often hear are:

1 "I don't need anything from them right now."
2 "I don't want to waste their time."
3 "They are busy people."

4 "I am going to wait until I learn more about the job or have a big win."

5 "I already know that person."

6 "I don't have time."

Remember that access comes with your role; if you don't use that access; you will not be viewed as operating at the proper level. Said bluntly—use it or lose it. You will miss out on the opportunity to fully embody your new role or take on the mantle of leadership that comes with the new position and time will pass you by. I have made this mistake myself.

When I was new to my role as quality systems manager, the general manager extended an open invitation because he viewed my role as key to the division's manufacturing performance. I thanked him and immediately dove into my work, making friends with colleagues but not leveraging the air cover the general manager could provide to accelerate the implementation of statistical quality control. When I finally reached out, I discovered that my general manager had resorted to (and now relied on) feedback from others. My warning to you: in the absence of direct feedback from you, others will use their access and fill in the gap. Don't let that happen.

> Luck is the sense to recognize an opportunity
> and the ability to take advantage of it.
>
> *Samuel Goldwyn*

It's also important to recognize that your value appreciates when you have the courage and confidence to utilize your unique abilities. Don't get distracted. Avoid the easy route of duplicating the efforts of others or getting caught up in activities that are important but don't move the ball forward.

Like Jay, you probably were awarded this opportunity because you have the intellect, talent, and communications skills to add to the organizational bench strength or to take on a future leadership role.

Don't delay! You may squander your social capital by making a wrong start, especially if you let your manager, co-workers and even your friends assume that you "know how to act." Time is important—ask your mentor for advice on how best to reach out if you are uncertain. Take a moment and consider the access your new position affords by listing the people you have access to. You can reach out, spanning

---

C-Suite Mindset

DO THE THING THAT ONLY YOU CAN DO

Advisor: Jay Tuli
Vice President, Leader Bank.
Named by Boston Business Journal as a Rising Star in Banking

Getting there at Leader Bank is all about hard work. I really worked harder than everyone else because I didn't have fifteen years of knowledge. I focused on adding value: researching ideas, doing grunt work, offering suggestions and finding ways to innovate. At first I didn't have a specific expertise. I didn't have to think about what I was doing every minute. Just work hard. Once people see that you have a good work ethic you get dumped with more responsibility.

Now, I have to be very thoughtful when I spend an hour on something: Am I doing the right thing, how am I spending this hour? Could someone else do it? I ask: What is the impact of the things that I need to do and are they pushing the Bank forward? I do the things that nobody else can do. Value is created if I can do X and Y, and if the other person can only to X, then I do Y.

---

organizational levels to touch individuals placed above and below you. Although most organizational charts look hierarchical, very few operate in a strictly formal manner because senior leaders realize that employees who are closer to the customer have the most accurate data about the organization's product, services and opportunities for improvement. When Howard considered the people that he had easy access to, he realized that the list included the president, major clients, a couple of senior vice presidents, and new peers in other organizations around the country.

Look again at the list of accessible contacts and consider any who may be missing in your situation. Now use the form below to fill in the name, job title and number of years the person has with the organization. Next, describe the immediate value the person has to the successful execution of your job and the value you provide in return. Have you developed your access to this person?

Now, as you consider how you will work together, rate (one to three stars) how well you know the person. Gauge the depth and breadth of your relationships. For example, three stars with a senior person means that you have met 1:1 (in person, by Skype or telephone) and that you know how your roles, expertise, experiences and networks fit together to be a resource or to achieve future goals. Rate someone on your own level as three stars if you know each other well inside and outside of business. If you see each other occasionally and have had at least one substantive discussion, rate your relationship as two stars; rate it as one star if you know each other only in passing. Don't make the mistake of believing you have a three-star relationship with a colleague just because you have worked together for seven years.

	Name	Title	Years	Value	***
Your manager					
Your manager's manager					
Your HR generalist or manager					
Your immediate team members					
Colleagues in your department or within your organizational function					
Clients, customers, vendors					
Administrative staff/resources					
Janitorial or cleaning staff					
Front desk personnel					
Competitors					

What does it take to maintain access?

One of the qualities at the very core of access is *reciprocity*. Consider whether you have reciprocal relationships with the people on your list. By *reciprocal*, I don't mean that you are their exact peers, in parallel spots on the organizational chart. I use two criteria to determine whether I have one-, two-, or three-star access:

1 Easy give and take: conversations that encompass mutual sharing of information, wide-ranging topics, and cordial disagreement.

2 Priority response: when I contact them, they get back to me, and when they contact me I get back to them right away.

Another critical part of tending the access relationship is *follow-through*: access only works if you follow through and follow up. For example, if a recommendation or idea comes up when you meet with a new colleague, follow through right away. Don't wait and mention it in your next conversation, let the person know that you followed through, then follow up by informing him of the outcome or next steps.

Indira neglected to follow up after using her access privileges, and it may have cost her her career.

> Promoted three years earlier to VP, Indira was feeling stuck and not challenged. She approached John, the head of her organization. Shortly thereafter, Indira interviewed with a half dozen people. John reached out to her during the interview process to ask if she needed any help or support. Indira said, "No thanks." Soon she was presented an offer to go to Singapore. Six weeks later, John heard that Indira had turned down the job.

Indira made a fatal mistake—she misused her access to John in several important ways. Can you name them?

1 Indira did not check in with John after their initial meeting.
2 When approached for the job, Indira did not ask John for his advice or perspective.
3 When John asked her if she needed help or support, Indira declined.
4 Indira did not advise John in advance that she was not going to accept the Singapore offer.
5 She allowed John to found out *through the grapevine* that she hadn't accepted the offer.

Just think: John used his access and influence to generate the opportunity for Indira. He put his social capital with key people in his organization on the line, and he probably assured them that Indira would be interested in the opportunity. What do you think will happen the next time Indira approaches a senior executive for help?

What is influence and how is it a perk?

To create the opportunity for Indira, John used his access and, more specifically, his influence. You know that you have influence when people listen to and then act on your ideas and recommendations or if they defer to your experience or expertise.

When you assumed your new role, you did so with the expectation that you would influence outcomes. But how? You have figured out by now that formal authority is overrated as a tool for getting things done. You may direct a team reporting to you, but don't over-use this authoritative approach. Let's face it, you can only delegate and direct a portion of your work. The way to succeed in organizational life is through cooperating and collaborating with others. Your ability to influence is what really extends your reach.

Influence is the tool that enables you to take advantage of your access. As you move up or laterally in your organization your ability to influence will be the key to your success. Through your influence, you can frame important issues your way, win support for your projects and ideas, and contribute to important decisions. Are you taking advantage of the sphere of influence your new role affords? Your influence depends on several key qualities, abilities, or knowledge bases, all of which you can develop further:

1 Your ability to analyze a situation quickly and accurately in a way that others are able to understand and make actionable

2 Your ability to assess the strategic impact or direction in measurable terms that others are able to understand and make actionable

3 Your credibility based on your record of success and accomplishments

4 Your access to the markets, to sources of information, to key clients and other sources of value.

You will derive the maximum benefit from your new role if you adeptly leverage your new access and influence to mobilize people and resources to meet and exceed organizational metrics. For example, consider the case of Evelyn, who took on a new role in a different part of the country. Very successful in her former position, Evelyn was skilled at putting out fires. But her new role required her to act proactively, to *make a case* for her point of view—that is, to use access and influence.

> The move was a culture shock, and the initiative moved really fast. Frankly, it's being rolled out too fast, and it goes to all levels from the Vice President to Chairman. I think that we lack the fundamentals—we should be more systematic.

Evelyn found herself getting to the boiling point before sending an "S.O.S." to her senior manager—and unfortunately she had not utilized her access to him to develop a relationship before the crisis hit.

> He has made all the right noises on the surface, but I haven't had any 1:1 with him yet. I am not in my boss's face—I don't have regular time with him. Generally, I try to operate transparently. I know the first step of the big plan, but there isn't clear direction about what we want going forward. I am just afraid with all the other initiatives that they will not see that this one is in trouble.

Evelyn stepped back from firefighting and recognized her mistake. She got on her manager's regular calendar. She expanded beyond her team to meet with all the people on her access list. She took advantage of her access and introduced herself to her new sphere, showing off the qualities that would make her influential in this environment. After all, her knowledge, track record, and strategic thinking were why she was hired for the role.

> I realize that we can be a world-class institution. Our department is key to attaining that goal. It's up to me to convey what needs to happen and to start pushing to get it done.

Will you use it, or lose it?

When you get to your new role, be aware of the access and influence you have: the perks of your job. If you don't use your access and influence you will lose out. On the other hand, the more you use your access and influence the more they will grow, solidifying your ability to contribute at this level and preparing the ground for your next move up.

Add your thoughts and ideas below:

	Questions	Yes/No	Actions
ALERT?	• Have I thanked the people who helped me get here and introduced myself to new colleagues? • Do I have a list of the people with whom I have access? • Have I identified the immediate value I can provide to them and they offer to me?		
ADJUST?	• Have my mentor and I discussed the best way to utilize my access? • Have I prioritized my list?		
ALIGN?	• Do I know how my work plan and immediate deliverables will influence results? • Am I taking advantage of the perks that come with my new role?		
ACT?	• Have I scheduled the appropriate meetings within the first 90 days? • Am I deepening my relationship with people I rated two stars? • Am I developing a relationship with those I rated one star? • Am I nurturing the relationships I rated three stars?		

What Practices Have
You Stopped? Started?

Are you there? Or are you on your way? You should have a definite yes or no answer. The exercises that you have completed allow you to be alert to the gaps between where you are and where you want to be, the adjustments you need to make in order to be aligned to your current or future organizational reality, and the choices and actions you will take. In other words you now have a plan.

But if you just read through the exercises and didn't write anything down, then you are approaching this the same way you approach other "self help" books. I warned you about the fallacy of this approach: thinking is not the same as doing. I am sure that you know that there is a big difference between watching your favorite cooking show or reading *National Geographic* and actually making the dish or taking the trip.

I remind you again: Thinking is not the same as doing. If you skipped over the exercises and questions and kept all of the information in your head, you are not actively engaged. You will not change your behavior by thinking about it. There is no magic wand, no easy out—you have to do the work. You have to be engaged with the process and make sense of the questions by considering how they relate to your unique situation. After you become alert to your current situation you can then commit to action. You can weigh the benefits of maintaining the status quo or committing to new approaches, styles, and behaviors. When you are in alignment, you can consider an array of actions that could move you toward your goal—you can choose the appropriate action based on the situation. But there are no short cuts. The steps are common sense but rarely common practice.

Getting there requires being prepared. Preparation and planning increase your agility. You will have choices available only if you have identified them in advance.

> When new turns of behavior cease to
> appear in the life of an individual,
> its behavior ceases to be intelligent.

Thomas Carlyle

When you write down your behavior you can analyze it and determine how or if it serves you. You will decide to *stop* doing some things, *start* doing others, and *continue* with those actions that lead you toward your goal. Your first goal is to be alert and aware of behaviors that are impeding your effectiveness or progress and to stop doing them now. You can only stop the behavior when you can write it down in observable terms and become accountable for it to yourself. When you see it in black and white you can assess how this behavior has gotten you this far—it has served you well—but now it simply isn't sufficient or appropriate. It is worn out, bankrupt. Commit to adding new tools to your tool kit to take the next step. You have identified the benefit of doing so and now you are ready to choose the right tool for the task at hand. If you play golf you know what I mean: you survey the terrain and select the right club. In other words you are employing new practices and take

---

C-Suite Mindset

BE ALERT AND ADAPT

*Advisor: Jim Padilla, retired from Ford Motor Company
as the President and COO after 40 years
and 25 very different roles*

I stayed in each role one to three years. You have to have a high degree of adeptness to jump on new assignments and climb on board. It is real important to make a quick start. Not every situation is the same. You have to evaluate: be perceptive— where are the strengths and weaknesses? Where do you have to bolster the operation? Quickly assess the people that you have. You may have a different set of skills and need a different set of people. Take the time and focus on the team because 99 percent of the situations are collective outcome. Get them pulling together fast. Walk the talk; hold them accountable— no micromanaging. Always, plan your work and work your plan—day in and day out.

C-Suite Mindset

STAY FLEXIBLE AND CONNECTED

Advisor: Stephanie Fritz
Talent Development Manager

Always be flexible and think about your career in a broad way. Be flexible and open to opportunities that may not be in your plan. Since age five I wanted to be a teacher. I only applied to one college because I thought that was what I wanted to do. When I got there I realized I hated it. I learned a lesson: Don't pigeon hole yourself. So, right after college I said, "What can I do? I am going to try different things." My teaching skills were transferable to a learning and development role, which I loved.

When offered an opportunity to leave my previous organization, I decided to open my own business back in my hometown of Philadelphia. There I discovered few opportunities and little interest in what I was offering. When a classmate from a course I took at Columbia told me about a job in NYC—well, I never pictured myself in Manhattan and in the tech industry, but I made the move. Staying flexible and doing my best has gotten me here. And, I have always, always built good relationships and a connection to my organizational community. To be really good at your job you have to build relations with people. To stay there, be flexible.

---

actions that allow you to produce consistent results and give you the confidence to take on new tasks.

Remember: there is always a "skills gap." Whether you are in a new role, or simply recognize that your environment is changing, something will always be "missing." You can fine-tune some areas but you will have to change others more dramatically. Always start with the low-hanging fruit—the changes that are easy to implement—and practice with the least risky audience (friends, family, mentors).

OK—I will give you a second chance to capture your insights and actions. Answer these questions: What is standing in the way? What actions have I taken? Now, be brutally honest and determine what you will stop, start and continue to do. Here is an example:

Stop:

- Playing "small"
- Being the "smartest person in the room"

Start:

- Maximizing my access/visibility
- Socializing my ideas
- Leveraging my strategic thinking
- Saying "thank you"

Continue:

- Mentoring and helping others
- Being fun to be with
- My commitment to personal and professional excellence
- Doing extraordinary work
- Expanding and deepening my network
- Making a difference for my customers

Keep your eye on the ball. Be prepared. Practice agility. Ask yourself the tough questions. Your "soft skills," behavior and style will determine your long-term success. And remember, there are different requirements for getting there and staying there. What do you need to stop? Start? Continue?

Stop:

- _____
- _____

Start:

- _____
- _____

Continue:

- _____
- _____

Staying There

*Don't ask yourself what the world needs; ask yourself what
makes you come alive. And then go and do that. Because what
the world needs is people who have come alive.*

— Howard Thurman —

What is Staying There? In a word, staying there is *success*. It is the result
of the actions you have taken to craft your next opportunity and reach
your goal with the support of an engaging and encouraging network.
Staying there is not a destination; you may position yourself for your
next move, which you will make in a manner and time of your own
choosing. If "Getting There" focuses on ensuring that your skills, knowledge, capacity are recognized and rewarded, by contrast "Staying There"
helps you find and polish the one additional thing you need and want
to hone to prove that you have it all together or to satisfy your personal
sense of accomplishment. You are at a point in your career where you
have moved from job to career to professional identity. You have choices
that are best for you and your family. For me, it's always the challenge,
the opportunity to grow, and the moment to bring everything together.

Once you achieve the opportunity you have worked for, you begin
to address the dynamics of staying there. When you first assume the new
role, both you and your manager or board know that you are a work-
in-progress—what makes the opportunity energizing is that it is a bit of
a reach. The organization has invested a lot in you already, whether in
recruiting you or grooming you through the ranks. Someone has stuck
his or her neck out to support your appointment. They see the seeds of
success or they wouldn't have selected you. But acknowledge that you
do still need to grow in order to maximize your current opportunity.
Staying there is not for the fainthearted—it can challenge everything
you know and cause you to become a better (different) person. Staying
there is arriving at your decision point—your personal Rubicon. Make
it your choice and drive for success in your career.

The move from getting there to staying there is a move from tactical to strategic thinking. Getting there is the reward for delivering; staying there is your reward for "fit," embodying leadership and nuanced behavior appropriate for the times and your organization's culture. It recognizes your developing mastery, from the tangible to the intangible, from the "what" to the "how."

Remember the qualities of agility:

1 Be alert, and recognize what is different about this new situation.
2 Adjust. Adapt your thinking to meet the new conditions; think strategically, not tactically. (For example, don't sell, instead look at the portfolio for an emerging market; develop others into the rainmakers).
3 Align your thinking and your network with the new expectations.
4 Act. To stay there, you have to tweak, adjust or outright drop bankrupt behavior.

It's a cycle. Once you get there, you stay there until it is time to move, to get to a new *there*. You will climb this spiral staircase, cycling through many times. As you move from getting there to staying there and back again, you'll see the same challenges facing you, often in different guises. Remember the Judy Collins song, "I've looked at life from both sides now…." She concludes: "I really don't know life at all." If that energizes you—if you are willing to step out on the long skinny branches—you have the right attitude to stay there.

Success!

Material success! Worldly success!
Personal, emotional success!

The people I consider successful are so because
of how they handle their responsibilities to other
people, how they approach the future, people who
have a full sense of the value of their life and
what they want to do with it.
I call people "successful" not because they have
money or their business is doing well but because,
as human beings, they have a fully developed
sense of being alive and engaged in a lifetime task of
collaboration with other human beings—their
mothers and fathers, their family, their friends,
their loved ones, the friends who are dying,
the friends who are being born.

Success!

Don't you know it is all about being able to extend
love to people! Really. Not in a big, capital-letter
sense but in the everyday. Little by little, task by task,
gesture by gesture, word by word.

Ralph Fiennes, actor

9

Do I Understand
What Is Expected of Me Now?

*The first step in exceeding your customer's expectations
is to know those expectations.*
— Roy H. Williams —

Let me tell you a little more about my first executive opportunity. Promoted after just a few years with the company, I thought I had "arrived"! But after several months in my new role, I had to face the fact that things weren't going well. I wasn't fitting in with my new—all older male—colleagues. I wasn't accomplishing much with my new staff: Having acted before learning the group's history, I bet on the wrong members of the team. Unfamiliar with the delicate give-and-take found at the executive level, I became a bull in a china shop. I skipped lunch because I had so much "work" to do. I asked probing questions at leadership meetings, only to see my colleagues look at me as if I had passed gas.

Organizations are often pictured as pyramids, and I was sliding down that slippery, sloping side! I had reached the executive suite but, like many people when faced with challenges beyond my knowledge, I retreated into the behavior that had worked in the past—the behavior that had gotten me there. I thought, "Well, they promoted me because they think I am good at my job, so I will just become even better at it!" I worked harder, not smarter, my desperate actions causing even more damage to the crockery. I racked my brain to figure out what was wrong, why it wasn't working. I know now what I didn't know then: When you are not meeting the expectations of a new situation, you must ask yourself, "Am I seeing the whole picture?" and, since the answer is almost always *no*, ask "What am I missing?"

C-Suite Mindset

YOU MUST INSPIRE

Advisor: Carolyn Chin
Corporate Board member and Co-founder of "OnBoard Bootcamps"

I find that many CEOs don't have an inspirational answer when I ask, "Where we are going?" They seem to answer, "We are going to move the dot a little." That is not what people want—especially the millennials. You can't tell me that you want to grow 10%; you have to be specific: What space do we want to specialize in? Who are we going to serve? To say we are going to double our sales in five years—what does that mean? That's not inspirational. Maybe you could quadruple your sales.

You have to inspire people. Even if the picture is far out— you have to show incremental steps of success. If it is a long haul, pick short-term goals. You have to have successes. This is hard work and people do the hard work because they are inspired.

Do you know what is expected of you in your new role?

When you are in a new role, it's easy to miss vital information or inputs. You may not have noticed that the view is very different from this new vantage point. You may be focusing on some things to the exclusion of others, or focusing on the wrong things altogether. When you assume a new position you can be sure of one thing: the expectations of your new role are not "more/faster of the same." They are *different* from what was expected in your old role. Before you can even ask yourself if you are meeting the expectations of your colleagues and superiors, you must first ask yourself: Do I understand what those expectations are? Of course you are expected to "get the work done"—that is a given. But what are the unspoken expectations? If you are at the helm it is time to lead.

How do expectations change
when you take on a senior role?

When you start out in your career, the expectations are all about delivering results. At the beginning, you deliver through your own efforts. Later, when you assume a supervisory or management role, you are expected to deliver results through the efforts of your staff. You learn to organize and motivate others to ensure that objectives are met or surpassed. You learn to communicate effectively, both with the people who report to you and with your manager and others above you in the organizational hierarchy. In order to succeed at this level, your behaviors—and the decisions that guide them—are *tactical*. They are focused on selecting and implementing the means to obtain your objectives. By being successful, you create an opportunity to showcase your competence, confidence, and capabilities as you prepare for the next level.

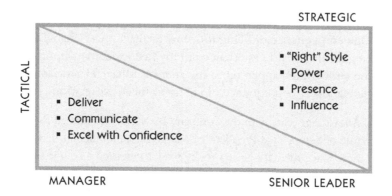

But when you reach that destination, the game changes, as summed up in the figure above. The more senior your role, the more *strategically* you are expected to think and behave. That means that you are expected to set the direction and determine the objectives that will define success for your organization. The higher your position, the more likely you will make decisions based on imperfect information. To be strategic you have to be alert and put your individual and collective experiences together. You use your authority and the power of your new role to motivate, inspire and create a compelling work environment. You have the "presence" befitting your stature in the organization that meshes with the "style" of your organization. Only if you behave according to these expectations will you be able to use your influence to form collaborative relationships and get things done across organizational boundaries.

Am I changing fast enough to accomplish what I need to accomplish in my position?

Moving from a tactical to a strategic mindset is a major change in attitude and behavior, and it may seem as though you have to make this shift overnight. Of course, if you have been preparing for your new position in the right way (following the precepts outlined in this book!), you have already begun to adopt a strategic point of view. In fact, your superiors have noticed this and it is probably one factor in the promotion you received. Still, big changes are in order:

- From "checking the boxes" to setting the agenda
- From directing to leading
- From accomplishing to establishing
- From following a path to blazing a trail
- From managing change to anticipating the "new new" for your sector

One consequence of being too slow to make these changes is that "sinking feeling" that I experienced in my first executive opportunity. I saw the same thing happening to my client Raphael. He was in danger of facing another consequence of failing to meet expectations:

> After seven years with the company, last year I was offered the role of Senior Vice President of Marketing in a different division. Since then, it's been a rocky road. I inherited a couple of failing campaigns and a few key people jumped ship. I've been having trouble getting approval for a new initiative I want to launch. Now reorganization is in the works and suddenly I look around and see competition for my own role!

If Raphael's superiors had wanted to watch those failing campaigns crash and burn, they would have left his predecessor in the role. But Raphael is playing out the old hand—tactically trying to meet the objectives of the old campaigns—instead of leading in a new and successful direction. He needs to take the strategic view: Decide what his objectives should be, dump the failing campaigns and launch new ones, assess his staff and make sure the best players want to stay on his team. If Raphael doesn't rise to meet expectations, he could find his career stalled.

> I don't really know the senior people here well, but I discussed the problem with my old boss. He pointed out that a lot of money has already been invested in the old approach; maybe I should just double down and make it work.

Red flag alert! Raphael has not gotten to know his new peers and the management team in his new division. As a result, he has no influence. To repeat a lesson from an earlier chapter, he isn't using his new access. And he is listening to the wrong people!

Make sure you are listening to the right people and asking the right questions. Don't ask the easy questions; instead, be like former Director of the Federal Bureau of Investigation William H. Webster. Ask the pointed questions. Ask the question that opens a new way of looking at the situation or exposes the flaw in the logic. Ask questions that come from the overall perspective, not the ones that nibble at the edges.

Do I understand the culture of how business gets done in my workplace?

One major expectation of any person in a senior position is that he or she will understand the culture of the organization and follow the unwritten "rules of the road." An organization's culture goes far beyond "casual Fridays." Don't get caught up in the cultural window dressing; pull the curtain back and pay attention to the who, what and how of decision-making! Work gets done because someone made a decision; things don't happen willy-nilly or by default. Focus on how work gets done, including these important manifestations:

- Who talks to whom. Whose ideas are reinforced? Whose are ignored?
- Where decisions are really made. Sure, major topics are discussed in management meetings, but the real decisions are often determined somewhere else.
- How power is exercised. Access? Information? Invitations? The organization chart may show that two position have equal sway, but one is almost always more powerful and influential, either because of personal characteristics or because of the value of the role itself.
- How disagreements are resolved. Are disagreements hashed out in honest and direct arguments, or do dissembling and backroom methods win the day?
- How decisions are made. Public, private, in advance of meetings or after?
- How decisions are executed, or not. Even *if* a decision is made, some companies go through an elaborate planning and budgeting process, only to make an across-the-board allocation increase or cut rather than actually placing a bet.
- How resources are allocated. Who sits at the head of the table? The real limits of your authority: what you can "really do now that you have this job."
- How coalitions are formed. Who are your allies and adversaries?

You may not be expected to know all these cultural realities on your first day, but you are expected to learn them, and fast! You will not succeed if you do not.

For example, why hasn't Raphael succeeded in obtaining the funding necessary for his new initiatives? One reason is that he has not "socialized the ideas" among his new peers, building coalitions among those who would support it, either because it would benefit them or because they owe him a favor. Raphael hasn't even acknowledged the quid pro quo associated with moving a project forward.

Can unspoken expectations be challenged?

What if you don't like the invisible expectations of your new role? You may think you can accomplish more by working your way rather than their way. Think again. If you are on the court, you are in the game and culture—national, ethnic, or organizational—is deeply engrained. Your first task is to understand and appreciate the game.

It is almost impossible for one person to change the game or the expectations that it fosters. Consider the case of Princess Masako of Japan. The daughter of a Japanese diplomat, Masako attended both Harvard and Oxford Universities. She was preparing to enter the diplomatic service herself before she married then–Crown Prince Akihito, only to learn that the expectations for her role were few and simple: smile, and produce a male heir. Her activities and travel severely restricted by protocol, Princess Masako has fallen prey to what the Imperial Household calls "adjustment disorder." Despite her intelligence and training, she has not succeeded in changing the expectations of her role. Hillary Clinton ran into similar, if less draconian, obstacles when she challenged the expectations of American First Ladies by becoming active in health care policy development.

Let these extreme cases serve as a warning. Learn the culture of your organization and adopt it if you want success in your new role. You may be able to make gradual changes in the future, but don't alienate yourself and become a stranger in a strange land. Your task now is to live up the expectations of your stakeholders. Be curious, ask questions—stay alert.

Who are the stakeholders and what is their relationship to me?

In addition to a new set of responsibilities, a new role brings new stakeholder groups. Unsurprisingly, not all the stakeholders hold the same expectations for you! Consider what each of these stakeholders expects of you in behavior, accomplishment, and attitude in your new situation:

- Your new boss
- Your boss's boss
- Your new staff
- Cross-functional and cross-organizational peers
- Your former co-workers
- Your family

Now consider how accurately you can define and satisfy their expectations.

Are my own expectations the enemy of my accomplishments?

There is another stakeholder that it is all too easy to overlook: yourself. What are your own expectations? And, important, are your expectations for yourself undermining your efforts?

We've all known people who can't take criticism. If you're reading these words, you almost certainly aren't one of them. High achievers at your level have understood from the beginning of their careers the importance of listening to and learning from the informed critiques of their colleagues and supervisors. In fact, it's one of the reasons they are high achievers. But are you one of those people with the opposite problem: you can't take praise? That's far more common among people who expect much of themselves and are dissatisfied with anything less than perfection.

I confess: I used to be like that. In fact, I was well into adulthood before I realized that what I dismissed as merely "OK" performance on my part was considered exceptional by others! Worse, when friends, mentors or bosses praised the results of my work, I was so thrown by the attention that I would reflexively downplay my achievement. Rather than enjoying my success, I would fix my eye on my next goal. Then, when I met *that* expectation, I minimized my achievement again, moved the bar up a notch and began reaching for the goal beyond that.

> I have very high expectations of myself.
> I'm a very competitive person but competitive
> with myself. I want to be the best that I can be and
> if that means that I'm eventually better than
> everyone else then so be it.
> *Wentworth Miller*

In my work as a coach, I see many of my clients with high expectations caught in this same vicious cycle. Their current performance is already stellar and *they* are the only ones who don't see it.

High performers generally love feedback. But for some of us, that applies only to criticism, not to praise. When the boss says, "That was great work!" the praise-averse achiever deflects the kudos with a shrug or "I was just doing my job." Privately, they may be thinking even more negatively. For example, after closing a very big deal, one of my clients told me, "Everyone thinks I'm so great. I haven't done anything in my life. I should be doing more."

Don't get me wrong. People who want to reach the peak of their profession can't afford to rest on their laurels. But not accepting praise is ultimately every bit as counterproductive as not taking criticism. Senior managers often apply the catchall phrase "lack of confidence" to people who consistently deflect affirmative feedback and continue to work harder and harder, well past what the boss needs or asks for. That lack of confidence can sidetrack or stall a promising career. Over time, it can make the most talented achievers think they aren't measuring up to the positive perceptions of their managers and friends. In turn, it can create the impression in others that you just aren't listening to them or valuing their opinions—and in fact, you aren't.

Don't let your own high expectations become your Achilles' heel. Here are some ways to make sure that you don't.

- If there's someone whose opinions you respect when they criticize your work, remind yourself of that respect when they praise what you do.
- Recognize that you are being appreciated because you delivered at a level of excellence when compared to your peers.
- Avoid undermining the value of your accomplishment by saying—or thinking—"That was nothing."
- Say "thank you" with enthusiasm when your boss, colleague, clients and friends acknowledge you and your work. Let them know that you genuinely appreciate their reaction.
- Don't reflexively "move the bar." Focus on excellence, not on "topping yourself."

And finally, when you complete a task, take a little private time to quietly appreciate your accomplishment. You are like a mountain climber, constantly moving towards a distant summit. But don't always look at what lies ahead. As mountain climbers do, pause every now and then and take a look at how far you have travelled, especially when you reach a milestone. Such moments will give you renewed energy and enthusiasm for the next leg of your journey.

Now it's your turn. What have you learned about the expectations surrounding your new role? To get a quick start, remember to pick the low-hanging fruit.

	Questions	Yes/No	Actions
ALERT?	• What's new or nuanced about the culture? • Do I know whom to ask? • What am I missing?		
ADJUST?	• Am I fitting in or floundering? • Are my own high expectations sabotaging me? • Are there any missteps to correct?		
ALIGN?	• Am I meeting expectations? • Are my priorities "right"? • Am I utilizing my access, influence and power appropriately? • Do my decisions have weight?		
ACT?	• Do I have a mentor to help me navigate the culture? • Are my communications flowing? • Am I able to be authentic?		

10

How Do I Lead?

Never look back unless you are planning to go that way.
— Henry David Thoreau —

At last, the Board had approved Eduardo's appointment to Regional Division Head. After the meeting, Eduardo went into his corner office, closed the door, put his feet on the desk and…basked. For exactly three minutes. "That was nice," he smiled. "Now, let's get to work!" Eduardo had already pondered the challenges of his new role, but he also recognized that the position afforded him opportunities to extend his leadership in different directions. Far from being a time to relax, when you reach a new position it is time to devote your skills, interests, and energies to forging *sustainable* leadership—an absolutely essential element of "staying there."

What is sustainable leadership?

You have probably heard the term "sustainable" a lot recently, but maybe not in the context of leadership. Yet the desired outcomes of sustainable leadership are similar to those of sustainable agriculture: to reap a bountiful harvest for individuals and organizations while preparing the ground for future and long-range success. Sustainable leadership is the capacity to adjust, align and maintain relationships and manage outcomes for continued success, achievement and accomplishment. Simply put, leaders sustain organizational success and continuity by inspiring employees and unleashing them to be their best. Employees give their all when they know their leaders won't let them down.

Leadership is a relationship between and among people. Leadership is increasingly being shared: co-leads, co-heads, regional partners, and multiple subject matter experts during the life of a project. But when the proverbial rubber hits the road, accountability, responsibility and attention often are fixed on one person: The leader. Leaders connect with and engage others. When you consider the multiple meanings of *sustainability*, a full array of actions can emerge. *Sustain* means:

1 To maintain, keep in existence
2 To keep supplied with necessities, to provide for, to nourish
3 To support from or as from below; to carry the weight or burden of
4 To strengthen the spirits, courage, etc., or to comfort; buoy up; encourage
5 To endure; to bear up against; withstand
6 To undergo; to experience; to support, as an injury or loss
7 To uphold or support the validity or justice
8 To confirm; prove; corroborate
9 To support in any condition by aid; to assist or relieve

From this perspective, companies are living ecosystems filled with individuals with unique needs and wants, who are most significantly compelled to be members of an organization in order to experience nurturing, nourishment, connection and community. Sustainable leadership! In what areas are you bringing the qualities of sustainable leadership to your role? As Mike Ullman advises: Everyone is a leader.

Are you holding on to the rope?

My friend Rollins has a saying: "Hold on to the rope." The metaphor comes from a story popularized by football coach Bobby Bowden:

> You are hanging from the edge of a cliff five hundred yards in the air. The only thing between you and falling to the ground is a piece of rope with the person of your choice on the other end. Who do you know that you can trust enough? Who do you know who has enough guts to withstand rope burn, watch blood drip from his hands, and still not let go?
>
> Look around and ask, "Who can I trust to hold the rope?' Who will let his hands bleed for me?" If you can look at every member of your team and say they will hold the rope, then your team will win!

Leaders who have developed themselves to the point where they embody sustainable leadership hold onto the rope for their organizations.

Holding on incorporates all the skills that you have honed to achieve your current level of success. Holding on taps the solid practices you have developed on three levels:

1 Your relationship with yourself. You continue to deepen or refine your self-awareness.
2 Your relationship with others. You are alert to the impact of your behavior (good and bad) on others.
3 Your relationship to change. Your interests, expertise and approach are not only executed appropriately but are also relevant.

By now, your skills in these areas are almost second nature. It is easy to relax and to stop strengthening these practices. It is easy to hand the rope off to someone else. At this point in your career, it takes *oomph* to want to keep doing more and getting better. Frankly, it is easier to double down on what you already know. But with that approach you will soon become obsolete; others will view you as outdated or inflexible and they will be right. They will see your lack of focus as you hand off the rope. Use your *oomph* to integrate and leverage your experiences by asking four questions: Am I relevant? Am I exploring new vistas? How effectively do I express my views? Am I actively expanding my perspective? Only by pursuing these objectives can you build sustainable leadership and hold on to the rope. You have to give to self before you can give to others. Refresh, renew or refuel to bring the same drive and passion to "staying there" that you brought to "getting there."

What do you do to stay relevant?

As you moved up the ranks in scope, accountability and responsibility, you learned that getting there and staying there don't follow straight-line paths. And as your career has taken steps forward, sideways, and even seemingly backwards, you have learned that you are good at some things and not so skilled at others. You are astute enough to recognize when you are making an impact and when your ideas fall flat. You have the experience, feedback and results to know what makes you relevant—what you offer that is unique, timely, and necessary.

Relevance is self-reinforcing: The more relevant you are, the tighter your grip on the rope. The tighter your grip, the more likely you are to sustain your relevance as a leader. Do the following paragraphs describe you? Answer yes or no.

- You read, attend conferences, ask questions and go beyond your comfort zone. As a matter of fact, you are energized as you incorporate new ideas into practice. You are recognized for your broad interests, you are engaged in your work, organization and community. You keep pace with the times, and you feel good because you are current and in sync with the issues of today. You don't try to know everything—it's not possible. However, you are interested, curious and open.

- You have a timely view and appreciation of a range of topics, from pop culture (music, fashion, the arts) to global issues (economy, international hot spots, human rights, climate change). Your values are not trapped in the 80s, 90s or the year you earned your degree. When someone asks, "Have you heard about....," you don't discount the topic just because it's not on your radar. You express curiosity: "No, tell me about...."

- Equally important, your skills are current. You keep pace with technology; no one would ever call you a dinosaur and your friends seek your advice on the latest apps. You are facile with social networking; you experiment with different devices undeterred by the learning curve—especially if your personal productivity is enhanced in the end. And, of course, you are current in your area of expertise and your contributions are pertinent to the issues at hand.

It's much easier to *remain* relevant than it is to *regain* relevance. And staying relevant gives you the confidence to branch out and pursue new objectives.

Are you an explorer?

Explorers know that there are opportunities beyond the horizon and they are willing to travel through unfamiliar places to learn about them. We admire individuals with the explorer's mindset: Steve Jobs, Stephen Hawking, Stephen Spielberg and my new favorite, J.J. Abrams. They are explorers not only by virtue of their innovative pursuits but also by what they learn about themselves on their journeys. You reached your current level of success because you have a rich body of experiences that define your perspective, influence your decision-making and give you the confidence to make decisions in ambiguous situations—that is, by exploring. Don't stop now.

The story of the 800-mile race between Captain Robert Falcon Scott and Roald Amundsen to reach the South Pole in 1910 is

C-Suite Mindset

EVERYONE IS A LEADER

Advisor: Mike Ullman
CEO JCPenney, Macy's

In my first job at the University of Cincinnati, I learned that there were no subordinates; that perspective has stayed with me. I learned to manage people differently by using what I brought to the table: I had resources and relationships that they didn't have. I learned that I could be successful and they could be successful. I had to be totally transparent and I put a huge focus on extreme communication. You cannot compartmentalize information. It is all about how the organization works. In a retail organization everyone has the same responsibility—selling and caring for customers. There are no subordinates.

My first year at Penney's, engagement culture survey results were 65. Only 90,000 of the 150,000 employees took the survey, but by my sixth year 93 percent took the survey and our engagement survey score was 91 percent.

How did we do it? My managers sat down with their teams and talked. We didn't go out and teach customer service. We focused on three things: Greet the customers, respect them while in the store and thank them. Remember that people don't like being told what to do: engage and respect the people you work with.

---

brimming with leadership lessons that are current today. Touring the *National Geographic* exhibit, I saw how differences in the men's experiences and approach predicted their survival or death; I was also struck by the role played by cultural expectations—that is, the expectations of their networks of supporters. Both Scott and Amundsen were men of towering ambition, and both rushed south to reach the Pole first. But four days after starting, Amundsen assessed his party's situation dispassionately and made the decision to

> "...hurry back to wait for the spring. To risk men and animals
> by continuing stubbornly once we have set off, is something I

couldn't consider. If we are to win the game, the pieces must be moved properly; a false move and everything could be lost."

Once underway, Amundsen built on his men's skill in skiing, and stashed plenty of food along the route. In contrast, Captain Scott:

> never learned to ski proficiently, so he and his men trudged, pulling their own sledges. Amundsen deposited three times the supplies Scott did; Scott starved and suffered scurvy.

And, not to be overlooked are expectations, the context provided by each expedition's network of supporters:

> "In Norway there is very little tolerance for failure in expedi-tions," one historian says. "You go and you come back whole." The British, in contrast, emphasized the struggle, believing that character, not skill, would win out and that death was heroic— a view that would be judged irresponsible today.

Leaders inspire followers, and followers allow their leaders to lead. But leaders are shaped by their place and time. Your network sets the expectations for your leadership. Look back to Chapter 3 to ensure that you have the "right" network to sustain your success. Do their expecta-tions help or hinder you?

Richard Branson is a modern-day explorer; inquisitive, daring and innovative, he embodies the principles of sustainable leadership. Since his first business adventure at age 16, Sir Richard has taken his own path and inspired others to follow. His career history showcases his expansive mindset: building on his experience in a record store to create Virgin Records, then pioneering the megastore experience, and finally branching out to other industries. His business empire is rooted in his personal interests, including media, music, finance, envi-ronmental causes and the challenge of public space flight, all infused with his dashing style that exemplifies the Virgin brand, as detailed on the company website:

> Virgin Galactic is investing in cleaner space technology with a design that has transformed the safety, cost and environmen-tal impacts of access to space [....] Virgin Galactic also assists scientific research greatly enhancing our ability to understand climate change and determine appropriate strategies to miti-gate the impacts. There is also potential for science to address

diseases as well as aiding research into new materials for transportation, computing and biomedicine.

Sir Richard's leadership crosses boundaries—in effect, he leads in a way that eliminate boundaries. And like his business interests, his compassion has no boundaries. In 2007 he worked with Nelson Mandela and Desmond Tutu to assemble The Elders, a group of leaders who contribute their wisdom, independent leadership and integrity to tackle some of the world's toughest problems. Other members include Mary Robinson, Peter Gabriel, Jimmy Carter and the first woman Prime Minister of Norway, Gro Harlem Brundtland.

You may think, "Richard Branson is brash and self-centered: I don't like his style." But don't confuse the characteristics of all explorers with the personality of any one individual. No matter what his personal style, Sir Richard is authentic, daring and original. He has the emotional intelligence to be charming and diplomatic when he chooses to be. He is effective because he is multidimensional. Now is a good time to consider your own authenticity and ability to flex your styles. Exploration and experiences provide the fuel for sustainable leadership. It is not just learning about new things; in the process you learn about yourself, exploring your personal landscape. You sustain your leadership by expanding your repertoire of behaviors and style.

Do you express your ideas effectively?

When Susan Hockfield became the sixteenth president of Massachusetts Institute of Technology in 2004—the first woman in the role—she shared her vision with confidence and conviction, stressing the importance of exploring:

> I want MIT to be the dream of every child who wants to grow up to make the world a better place. We need to reach those young *explorers* and bring them with us on the great adventure of discovery and innovation.
>
> Science, math and engineering can give you the exhilarating power to become not mere spectators or consumers, but the *active explorers*, makers and doers who will help invent the future.

Sustainable leaders have the ability to express and convey their ideas authentically. Because they are so adept at making connections, people may dismiss their skill at self-expression as mere charisma: "You either have it or you don't." But skillful communicators like Susan Hockfield choose their words carefully. They know that the greater the clarity of expression, the more effective the connection will be.

Why is self expression so difficult for so many? It seems that very early in life people define themselves as good communicators or bad. They are "good" public speakers or "bad" ones, either at ease with strangers or fumbling with what to say. But the key to effective communication doesn't lie in your comfort level; it lies in the clarity you bring to your thinking and the firmness of your intention to communicate. Your communication will go nowhere if you are convinced that you have nothing to say, or that you are confused or that you will forget and make a mistake. Don't start a conversation digging yourself out of a hole of doubt. Set your feet firmly on the ground and take a deep breath. The capacity to express your ideas clearly and succinctly can be yours if you can do three simple things:

- Be clear about the point you want to convey
- Define *how* your ideas may be of interest or relevance to others, and
- Always know *your first and your closing sentences.*

I often ask my clients, "If you are not interested in or clear about what you are saying, why do you think your audience should listen?" Rather than getting stuck in the details of the words you plan to say, be clear about what you want to communicate. What difference will your message make to your team, to your organization, to a body of knowledge or to the world? My clients who are introverts are always pleasantly surprised to find the gravitas behind their speech: unlike their extrovert peers, they don't talk all of the time. When they do, people listen. For example, Alison told me:

> My tendency is to be quiet in the beginning when I meet people—I tend to open up later. It takes longer for people to know me than it should and I may miss an opportunity to get to know people. I have a new role and what excites me about this opportunity is that I work with individual clients. They respect me and my presentation went well. Actually, my manager gave me phenomenal feedback.

Sustainable leadership encompasses more than expressing your own ideas effectively. Sustainable leaders also assist and encourage others to understand and share them. The more people there are who understand

and voice your ideas, using the vocabulary you have defined, the wider your influence will reach.

You should also encourage others to express themselves, because when self expression is snuffed out or smothered, organizations suffer: productivity goes down, costs go up due to errors and employee turn-over, and innovation tapers off. Makes sense: if you can't be yourself at work how can you be your best? You might be surprised to learn that a statistician—the founder of the quality movement, Dr. W. Edwards Deming, had keen insight into the factors that suppress authentic self-expression. He catalogued the forces of destruction beginning with the forced distribution of grades in school and continuing to the competition among people, groups and divisions as they attempt to meet quarterly targets and goals.

> One is born with intrinsic motivation, self-esteem, dignity, cooperation, and curiosity, joy in learning. These attributes are high at the beginning of life but are gradually crushed.

Dr. Deming's comments were prescient at the time and they serve as a wake-up call now because the same forces of destruction are still at work. Dr. Deming's wisdom continues to guide my coaching approach. If you believe (as I do) that the best way to sustain organizational success and continuity is to inspire and unleash employees to be their best, then it is up to you to eliminate the factors that crush self-expression so that curiosity, risk-taking and innovation can flourish.

For example, when Eduardo looked around at his management team, he understood that to make the group more innovative he had to encourage more freedom of expression than his predecessor had allowed. He began to subtly encourage healthy disagreement in senior meetings.

> At first they didn't take naturally to the idea that it was a good thing to disagree with me. I actually had to "stage" a scene with Elaine, where she disagreed with me and survived—even succeeded in changing my mind!—before they began to emerge from their shells.

He also changed the compensation plan to increase senior management's joint accountability for success and failure of the organization.

> There were some howls of protest about that! But the end result was that everyone really gives their best thinking to every proposal, not just advocating for their own turf.

Is your worldview always expanding?

When I asked my friend Barbara to describe me, she said, "You have never met a person that you didn't learn from," and, "Your joy in life is contagious—people like being around you." (*"Thank you"* is what I coach my clients to say—don't deflect the compliment!)

Are you always learning? There are countless opportunities to expand your thinking, your perspective, your knowledge, how you relate and the work you want to do. There are countless opportunities to see the world differently through the eyes and experiences of the people you meet. When my friend Beatrice boarded the plane from Paris to Boston, her seatmate looked at her and said, "We have six hours; I hope that you are interesting." What would your response have been? Well, Beatrice said, "I was just thinking the same thing!" and they simply started talking about their work, their loves, their losses and their dreams. (Note: When you see me on the airplane, don't expect the same response. I am the person with the eyeshades and earplugs, sleeping!)

> Change is inevitable; growth is optional.
> *John Maxwell*

Business leaders must expand too. Most people know something about Mark Zuckerberg from the movie *Social Network*. Not all the facts are accurate, but it's likely that Zuckerberg would admit that the film captured his nerdy and introverted style, almost painfully on display in his 2010 interview with Diane Sawyer. But as Facebook has expanded, so too has Mark Zuckerberg. As the "face" of Facebook, today his communication is crisp and he exudes confidence. He has never wavered in his vision and leadership of the company. Imagine the fortitude he displayed, resisting mega-million-dollar offers from Google, Yahoo and Microsoft as Facebook grew. Showing unshakeable focus, Zuckerberg took Facebook public in 2012.

In a May 2012 interview with *New York* magazine entitled the "Maturation of the Billionaire Boy-Man," Zuckerberg admits his youthful gauche behavior, but

> "If you're going to go on to build a service that is influential
> and that a lot of people rely on, then you need to be mature,
> right.... I think I've grown and learned a lot."

Many innovative companies go under because their leaders aren't able or willing to grow, let go, or expand their approach. The demise of "solid" New England firms Digital, Polaroid, and Wang are chilling examples. In contrast, according to the *New Yorker* interview:

> When early mistakes risked an employee mutiny, Zuckerberg knuckled down and learned how to lead. He made himself the pupil of some of the best bosses in business but had the maturity never to let outsiders sway his overall vision. He got adept at hiring the right people, and, more important, firing senior employees whom the company had outgrown.

Zuckerberg was not just interested in getting better as a leader; the network of leaders he assembled called him a "sponge." I wonder, given that you are at the top of your game, are there areas in which you have an unstoppable desire to improve? Consider: In what areas would you be a "sponge"? Would this make you a more effective leader?

The best way to realize your capacity to be expansive is to engage your network of friends, colleagues, mentors and advocates. The value of your network is determined not by its size but by its responsiveness and honesty. What good is it to have 1,000 Facebook friends or LinkedIn contacts when you don't have relationships with them? You can tell from Mark Zuckerberg's intensity that his real-life friends mean more to him than a number. Define your network by the friends and colleagues who "have your back" (or who you trust to hold your rope). I recommend creating a visualization of your network: Use Pinterest to compile a collage plotting your friends' geographical locations. I use a tried-and-true technique: I array photos on windows, bookshelves and an old-fashioned corkboard so I can see them and think about them every day. Bottom line: Make your social network visible and accessible. The depth of our relationship and commitment to each other means that we stay in touch on a regular basis, whether it's daily, weekly, and monthly or on special occasions.

Creating sustainable leadership means to keep something going, to continue leading or contributing at your level. In the process you are nurtured, nourished and inspired and as you lead your vibrancy will ignite others.

Are you ready to lead? Consider the questions on the following page. Add your thoughts and ideas:

		Questions	Yes/No	Actions
ALERT?		• Am I present and self-aware? • Do I take the time to connect to others? • Do I have something to say (contribute)?		
ADJUST?		• Do I know who "has my back"? • Do I prepare and practice before speaking?		
ALIGN?		• Do I have the right team in place? • Do I have buy-in and support?		
ACT?		• Is the department or organization "alive"? • Are people empowered and willing to share ideas? • Are we meeting and exceeding expectations?		

11

Why Am I in This Mess (Again)?

*Alice said: Would you tell me please, which way I ought to go
from here? That depends a good deal on where you want to get to,
said the Cat. I don't know where…said Alice. Then it doesn't
matter which way you go, said the cat.*

— Lewis Carroll —

In early 2011, the CEO of one of Boston's largest and most prestigious hospitals stepped down, his departure triggered by the scandal of a relationship with a female employee. Paul Levy wrote about the experience in his memoir:

> You are probably wondering how I could have been so foolish as to have misjudged the situation that caused all this strife. It turns out that this is a common disease of CEOs and other leaders. When you are engaged in doing your job, and you know you are doing it well, you tend to rationalize away things that should be warning signs—things that you would immediately notice as poor judgment if some other leader were doing them.

That is one of the best definitions of a personal blind spot I have ever seen. Levy managed to ignore quite an elephant in the room! But don't think that you can relax just because the pachyderms in *your* parlor are less imposing and less potentially destructive to you and your organization!

As easy as it is to miss important information or perspectives about other people or external situations, you probably have more misconceptions about yourself than anything else. Like everyone, you have a blind spot—something you just can't "see" about yourself. Just as with visual blind spots, there is no dark "hole" warning you that you are missing something. The brain fills in for the ocular nerve's shortcomings, and in a similar way your mind hides your personal blind spots, which are always obvious to others, but, by definition, invisible to you. That's one reason that coaching conversations are so important.

Blind spots take many forms. Your blind spot may be a tendency to put yourself down, to resist data contrary to your desires, or to avoid conflict. Your blind spot may show up in a pet project that you protect far after its lack of value is clear to everyone else. The habit may be physical, such as an annoying laugh, or social, such as appearing arrogant by checking texts during meetings. Blind spots are not necessarily inherently bad traits, but as long as you are not aware of them you are at their mercy.

Although you can't see your blind spots, you can "catch them in the act" if you are alert. Blind spots show themselves through their effects, and they often surface as "problems" when you assume a new role. Let's examine blind spots to learn how to spot them and keep them from taking your career off the fast track.

Are you the victim of your own success?

You've heard the proverb, "When all you have is a hammer, everything looks like a nail." You are probably one of the best "hammerers" in your organization, or management wouldn't have selected you for promotion. But when conditions change, what had been a strength can become a liability. And because it's something you value and that has served you well in the past, that's the last place you'll look for the source of your trouble. But you are pitching fastballs in the bowling match.

A brilliant engineer, Tom had risen quickly in the organization. His technical acumen and his problem-solving ability were legendary; his name was on dozens of patents. Now he was ready—or thought he was ready—to move from engineering to the corporate side of the business. But he had a big problem: he considered himself the smartest person in every room.

> Most of the people I work with now aren't engineers—in fact, none of them are. So I spend countless hours—I waste my time—explaining why we can't do things. Why should I listen to them, when I already know what they are going to say?

His manager had a different take:

> Sure, he's the best engineer in the company—maybe in the history of the company—but he won't go any farther until he learns to listen and work with people.

The very thing that got Tom there—his technical expertise—was impeding his progress because it was interfering with developing the skills that were essential to the next level: listening and collaborating.

Truth be told, Tom was never a good listener, but until now he never had to be! His blind spot wasn't a problem until he wanted to move into a role where collaborative skills were essential to success. Tom had to leave old habits behind and develop a new portfolio of skills to meet the requirements of his career objectives.

> You'll either step forward into growth
> or step back into safety.
> *Abraham Maslow*

Any change in your circumstances calls for changes in your behavior, and if you persist in your old patterns you will find yourself in trouble. Paul Levy thought he could continue his old behaviors in his new role. He was wrong. Have you moved into a new position, only to find that your approach, style, or skills are no longer effective? Does it seem your career has "hit the wall"? What's going on here? As you move up in your career, you can always expect blind spots to surface. Once invisible, they are now jarringly apparent. The old habits or the winning formulas that earned you success in the past just don't work as well in your new role.

Are you having a déjà vu experience?

Another way you can glimpse your blind spots is by becoming aware of the recurring "situations"—usually unpleasant—that you find yourself in. They can tip you off to behavior patterns that you don't notice but that have consequences. Linda, who was eager to be made a partner in her architectural firm, was furious when she was passed over for promotion *again*. Recognized for her innovative designs and for her track record of bringing new clients into the firm, Linda received high ratings from her clients. But her colleagues found her "anti-social" and her boss thought (correctly!) that she had a big chip on her shoulder. Linda complained:

> It's totally unfair. I am head and shoulders more competent than my boss. I bring in the business, create stand-out designs, and make him look good. It drives me crazy when he gets up in leadership meetings and takes credit for "our" accomplishments!

Linda's attitude was about to cost her career. She was treating her customers much better than she was treating her colleagues and her boss. It didn't matter if she was right about being a better designer than her boss, her boss's competency wasn't being questioned. He wasn't trying to make partner—but Linda was! Individual achievements are great for individual contributors, but her blindness to the group's norms and requirements had prevented her from being promoted, again. Her blind spot would make trouble for her until she corrected it.

What is your blind spot?

Don't ask whether or not you have a blind spot—everyone has one, or many! The tip-off is that sinking feeling that you are going down the same maze route that never has cheese at the end, but you can't stop walking. Or, you notice that your expertise or approach is no longer effective, it is bankrupt, and its results are unreliable. If so, it may be time to ask, "What am I missing? What is my blind spot and how can I correct it? What am I not aware of in my behavior and choices, and how is it lowering the quality or consistency of my results?" Another way to ask these questions is, "Why do I make the same mistakes more than once?"

The answer is often a blind spot. Here are a couple of actions you can take to reveal your blind spots to yourself:

- Pay attention to what people are saying. If three people have commented on the same trait or behavior, either casually or in anger, consider that it is probably true, even if it seems impossible to you! "What, *me*? Short tempered?" If they say you walk like a duck, quack like a duck....

- Notice what irritates you most in others. It is a psychological truism that we dislike most in others what we cannot see in ourselves. When you say "I can't stand it when she...." or "I hate it when people are..." it's like a big red flag waving: "Look over here! This trait is in you, too!"

> Everything that irritates us about others
> can lead us to an understanding of ourselves.
> *Carl Jung*

- Be sure there are some contrarians in your crowd. If you surround yourself with yes-men and people who depend on your favor for advancement, you will never hear the truth.

C-Suite Mindset

ROUTINES KILL CREATIVITY

Advisor: Evelyn Barahona,
Director of Business Development, Quality Interactions

You cannot get there without doing the work. Management looks only at the end point and doesn't see the process. People get stuck on routines—routines kill creativity. Every once in a while, shake it up! Invest in executive coaching. It brings my thinking to a new level and helps me be organized and focused.

- Notice your thinking. How many times do you think or say "no" every day? What is easier to answer: what you want and like? Or what you *don't* want and dislike? What triggers fear or embarrassment in you? What makes you angry or annoyed? What topics do you avoid?
- Find the behavior you make excuses for in yourself. Blind spots often hide behind "important reasons." "Sorry I kept you all waiting, I had an important phone call" signals that you think your needs are more important than everyone else's—a common opinion when dealing with subordinates, but not a popular one among your peers.

What is keeping you from seeing your blind spots?

Rubin's vase is a drawing, often used to test perception, in which the edges of a vase are also the profiles of two faces looking toward the center. If you are familiar with it, you probably can "see" both the vase and the profiles. However, many people can only see one image; once they "lock in" on one, it becomes harder to see the other. This frustrating exercise illustrates our human tendency to see what we want or what we already know. We sometimes ignore new information, even if it is blindingly obvious.

Paul Levy, the hospital CEO whose story is at the head of this chapter, learned this lesson the hard way, when he convinced himself that he had all his bases covered.

I mean, I've had a practice over the years to hire people who would question all the time. And they did on substantive matters, on business matters, on clinical matters and all the rest. But I think in this particular case, because they viewed it as a personal issue, that they felt uncomfortable or felt that it wasn't appropriate.

Levy may have separated his personal and professional lives in his earlier roles, but he should have known that highly visible CEOs don't have this luxury. He hid his blind spot from himself by not inviting his staff to comment on *anything* that could damage his personal brand or the brand of his employer. (By the way, do you think that Levy still has a small blind spot, if he doesn't consider behavior that derailed his career and embarrassed his organization to be "substantive"?)

How will you go about correcting your blind spot?

Once you figure out what is going on, it's time to ask yourself: What do I want? and, What are my choices? As always, answering these questions honestly demands courage: you must recognize and take responsibility for your role and expectations in the current situation. You must be willing to take action, and alert to find the moment to do so.

Blind spots are anchored in place by patterns of behavior—routines. After you find the behavior that is the symptom of your blind spot, ask yourself what you could do differently when confronted by its trigger. If you chose to do something different from what you ordinarily do—what *could* you do? What would be the benefit? I don't recommend that you try to get to the "psychological root" of the problem. Instead, identify the choices you have. Instead of doing the usual thing, what could you do instead? Tom knew he had to gain the trust of his peers to meet the expectations of his new role.

> I see that I can be impatient when people don't come right to the point. I need to curb that and hear them out, even acknowledge that I haven't thought of everything. Because they aren't engineers, they don't know about the technical side—that's what I bring to the equation. But they do know about the market, and about the politics of the organization, and I am beginning to see the value of their experience.

The behavior stemming from your blind spot will limit your effectiveness, performance and relationships. It may be annoying to your boss or the board of directors. Linda had to give her boss and her peers the same courtesy and respect she gave her customers. Above all, she had to stop criticizing management so that she could become a member of management!

Tom and Linda used a couple of techniques you may find useful:

- Ask your friends to support you by reminding you when you are behaving the old way and by celebrating your triumphs. Tom asked a colleague to discreetly signal him if he interrupted a colleague or starting explaining why his peers were "wrong."

- Focus on *choice* not *change*. You aren't losing something; you're choosing other options. You are adding new tools to your tool kit, which will increase your agility. When Linda made an extra effort to interact positively with her boss and find ways she could add value, her boss noticed something "new" about Linda. Her choice—her new mindset—was easy to adopt: treat her boss the same way she treated her clients.

Changing the behavior around your blind spot may well be a requirement for your new role or level. In any case, you can be sure your blind spot is distracting from your leadership and credibility. Don't wait to get into the same old mess. You need to address it. Ask yourself the tough questions now.

To really avoid getting into the same mess again, now is a good time to go a step further and complete the following:

Stop:
- _____
- _____

Start:
- _____
- _____

Continue:
- _____
- _____

	Questions	Yes/No	Actions
ALERT?	• Do I ignore my friends or colleagues when they bring X to my attention? • When I already know the outcome—and don't like what I see—can I change course?		
ADJUST?	• Can I see how doing X creates an unnecessary hurdle? • Have I brainstormed options with a trusted friend or colleague?		
ALIGN?	• Do I have the right tool(s) in my tool kit?		
ACT?	• Am I taking the appropriate steps? • Are my behavior, style, and approach appropriate?		

12

Have I Adjusted My Thinking to the New Requirements of Leadership?

When you are through changing, you are through.

— Bruce Barton —

Four months into her new role, Sarah was taken off guard. Her team was jumping the gun, rushing to implement a solution that she was still considering among several options.

> I was just thinking out loud, tossing around a few possibilities. I didn't expect them to form a project team! I hadn't reached a final decision on the best way to go forward. But they are "off to the races!"

After she approved the plan, Sarah asked her boss for his opinion of the proposal.

> Bad idea! He almost snapped at me—"Why are you looking for my input on this? You're close to the problem, you've got the data, you've got the budget, and you don't need my approval to go ahead."

Like many people who have taken a big step up in scope and authority, Sarah had assumed new responsibilities and taken on a new staff, but she had neglected to adopt a new mindset that reflected the reality of her new position. New roles bring a new reality that is manifested in changing levels of authority, accountability and access. Imagine that your old role placed you on the 8th floor of your 30-story building, and your new role places you on the 26th floor. Take a look out the window at your new view: You can see further, see new patterns and new details appear between the sky and the pavement. Keep that perspective in mind as you think about leadership in a new way; it is obvious that you are no longer at ground level or in the weeds.

What's different about this new level of leadership?

When you move into your new role, the changes may not be obvious, so you must be open and alert to adjust your thinking appropriately. Be mindful—you are not in Kansas anymore! Although you are the same person, your team, colleagues and clients will begin to respond differently to what you say and do. Sarah stumbled over several signs of her new reality before she found her footing. In addition to launching an initiative before she was ready and being reprimanded by her boss for seeking his approval, she was taken by surprise when the board chair invited her to join the governance committee meetings. Luckily she stopped herself before stammering, "Me? Why?"

Sarah had a new title and a new role, but she didn't have a new mindset. For example, by letting her team mistake her "thinking out loud" musings for instructions, she was ignoring the reality that her words now carry more weight than they did before. She had not adjusted to her new *authority*. When her boss declined to bless her plans, he was not so subtly reminding her of her new *accountability*. And the invitation to join the governance committee spoke to her increased *access* to power within the organization.

From	To
Asking permission	Being in action
Giving input	Providing direction and asking others for input
Thinking out loud	Strategizing and communicating next steps
Accepting	Setting the tone
Waiting to be invited	Granting access to staff, having an open door
Focusing on content	Focusing on context and process to free employees to make decisions
Fixed and predicable	Ubiquitous and serendipitous

New levels of authority, accountability, and access require new thinking and new behaviors. What is the mindset shift or adjustment you need to make?

What is missing from this list for you? In what other areas do you need to adjust your thinking?

From	To

Jim Padilla began his career as a quality control engineer at Ford Motor Company. He gained increased responsibility and scope as he moved and grew through a series of management positions in engineering and manufacturing. He is fondly called the "Father of the new XJ6" for his leadership role in dramatically turning around and overseeing the successful launches of Jaguar XJ series, the Jaguar XK-8 and the world-class AJ26 engine, Aston-Martin DB-7, Jaguar S-Type. How did he do it?

C Suite Mindset

NEVER ADJUST YOUR PRINCIPLES

Advisor: Jim Padilla
Former COO of Ford Motor Company,
who led successful integration and turnaround of Jaguar

Quality was always pivotal to me. I never waivered—it was a fundamental commitment. There are no excuses for poor quality.

Are you still focused on the content of your role?

When you are in a new position it is natural to focus on your new responsibilities—the *content* of your role. But frankly, it is assumed that you have the content under control—that is why you received the promotion. The true key to appreciating and adjusting to your new reality is being aware of *context*. I often suggest that my clients draw a doughnut, put themselves in the center, on the next area write process and the outer circle "context." The *context* is the environment you must navigate both in your organization and in your industry.

If you have learned nothing else by reading this book, you know by now that diving into your work or getting buried in the task and concentrating on meeting your metrics will throw you off the path. (Yes, I deliberately mixed those diving, burying and throwing metaphors to grab your attention.) How you get to your goal—understanding the *process*—is more important than the goal itself. With the right processes in place, you can tackle any objective, and make a touchdown even when the goalposts move (to add another metaphor to the pile!).

Note that following a process, going step by step, isn't the same thing as using linear thinking. Linear thinking is like being on railroad track or being railroaded—it's automatic, predicable; it will keep you heading into a tunnel even though you see the headlight of an oncoming train. You wouldn't be where you are today if you led with linear thinking. By contrast, following a process is a good idea—breaking things into steps and communicating those steps to others is at the core of Six Sigma, LEAN, Balanced Scorecard and project management. Working closely with Dr. W. Edwards Deming, the father of the quality movement, I led improvements in both manufacturing and state government processes. Interestingly, psychologist Ellen Langer reached an appreciation for processes from a completely different starting point: not from a desire for statistical improvement but from her understanding of *mindlessness* and its corollary, *mindfulness*.

Like Deming and many others, Langer urges us to focus on process before outcomes. This is the real importance to you as a leader:

> People can imagine themselves taking steps, while great heights seem entirely forbidding ... A process orientation not only sharpens our judgment, it makes us feel better about ourselves. A purely outcome orientation can take the joy out of life.

Virgin Group provides an excellent view into this. Because the right processes are in place, Richard Branson can give his team the same freedoms that he relishes. Even when launching a business in new territories, normally a difficult and risky project,

We have a process that works very well. In Chile and Poland, teams assessed the needs and requirements of the markets, then structured the companies accordingly—there was no top-down pressure dictating how the companies should manufacture or sell their products and services, or otherwise conduct their daily business.

These employees aren't focused on the "content" or metrics (another word for profits). With the right processes in place, the objectives will be met and Branson doesn't let a short-term focus on metrics distract from innovation:

> Another of the areas where we ask many employees to make their own decisions—and many other brands can't— is short-term profit: We focus less on this metric than most companies do. We all understand the importance of profit— if we didn't, the Virgin Group would not be around long. However this shouldn't be, and never has been, our driving force. Our employees are free to take positive risks knowing that they will not solely judged on a company's profit margin, but also on factors that all of us at Virgin value, like raising awareness of the brand, creating happy and loyal customers, or making a positive impact on the larger community.

The *content* is the "what": your role and responsibilities—in this case, establishing offices in new countries. The *process* is the "how": the steps through which you fulfill your role and responsibilities by collaborating with others and/or mobilizing your team resources. Informed by Virgin's organizational culture and other components of the *context,* including the unique characteristics of Chile and Poland, the individuals called on processes that are key to the organization's success. Notice the processes in place in your organization; they are what bring your culture, defined as "the way we do things around here," to full expression and definition.

Viewing your organization from the direction of "context in" versus "content out" is an effective and targeted way to adjust your thinking. What is the context? Ask yourself, what are the environmental factors, technological changes, competitive landscape, economic pressures, demographics, buying patterns, energy prices and so on that have *or will have* an impact on your organization? An awareness of context prepares you to be nimble when change arrives, as it inevitably will.

C Suite Mindset

ALWAYS GO BEYOND

Advisor: Ben Olds
Talent Business Advisor, Deloitte

You need a unique approach. I do what I am asked and always go beyond. How? I am curious. I ask: What are you looking for? What will take it to the next level? I ask: What is the context? How will this analysis be used?

Here is how I think about it: Visualize a graph—there are dots arrayed in a linear relationship between the y and x axes. There is one dot outside the line: an outlier that is outside the trend line. A good performer would connect the dots. A great performer would draw a line— and circle the outlier. Complete the analysis about the trend and then explain the possible effects of the outlier.

Pay attention to the questions that you are being asked: next time you can ask them.

Are you ready
to face disruptive change?

The education industry is in the midst of an upheaval. In 2010, I discovered Khan Academy through a client who was intrigued by the technology of online learning and excited by its potential in the developing world. I immediately went to the site and undertook an in-depth review of financial accounting and a more leisurely browse through American history, for free. Two years later, Harvard and MIT announced their joint venture edX and in November 2011 the *New York Times* magazine featured the provocative image of a rabbit to illustrate the title: "Massive and Multiplying ...MOOC" (massive open, online courses). Coursera, edX , Udacity—all are online, open and free.

What is the disruption? How about that word: *free?* If tuition bills come to you, you automatically compare the cost of your own education in 1970-1998 to today's fees at a residential state school ($20,000 per year) or a private liberal arts college ($45,000)— fees three to five times greater than what you paid, for a college education may not require sitting in a lecture hall or even going to class. (One of my clients aced his courses by reading the materials and lecture notes online—he considered it the best use of his time, and managed to letter in three sports while earning an engineering degree at MIT. Perhaps the greatest benefit he received from residential college was his excellent time management skill!) What if, instead of that whopping bill, tuition was free?

If tuition is free, what will the financial model for online education be? Will students pay for a certification? Will the certification have the same cachet that a residential degree carries? What is the competitive landscape for colleges: who will survive and who will go under? According to Richard Vedder in *Forbes*,

> Traditional colleges at opposite ends of the glamour spectrum will probably survive. At one end, community colleges could deliver bankable skills in fields like nursing and computer network installation. At the other end, elite institutions like Princeton will carry on for a few more centuries. In between? "It's going to wipe out high-cost mediocre private schools without big endowments."

We can follow the connections into the future and speculate about how the funding model for colleges will change as parents and students balk at the inflation in tuition costs. Until now, colleges have been able to raise their fees again and again without a dramatic reaction, just as scientists can gradually heat a pot of water to boiling without causing a frog in the pot to leap out. Over the past 10 to 15 years, parents have taken out bigger loans to pay for rising tuition costs while unemployment and underemployment among recent college graduates is at record levels and President Obama and business leaders are bemoaning a skilled worker shortage. What if college becomes an à la carte experience study and pay for what you need, when you need it? How will your organization recruit and select new employees?

A disruption is underway and a stream of conversations will intersect. The point of this long example is, are you open to seeing change and anticipating its trajectory? Can you assimilate the context and plan a path and a process? As you read through the dynamics, you can see the interconnections—online delivery, value and cost to students and parents—and adjust your thinking to the new reality: education is on the brink of a disruptive change. The college infrastructure, online learning and payment systems, the value and credentials of skills, and the assumptions about what learning is and is not—are all related. We are moving from one mindset or system of thought to a new one. I find it intriguing and exciting—what about you? If you were a leader in the field of education, how would you act in this context?

What are the characteristics of context-focused individuals?

When you are aligned and in step with the current context—the reality of today—then you adjust your approach and style accordingly. *Forbes* selected the following characteristics to describe the 2013 "Thirty Under Thirty." Stop and think: Would others use these words to describe *you*?

	Yes/No
Disruptor	
Impatient	
Change The World	
Innovator	
Entrepreneur	
Creative	
Intellectual Best	
Surprising	
Engaging	
Fascinating	
Hard-Working	

If you answered, "yes" only to "hard working," you need to adjust your brand and style. You may be thinking, "But my job, my role doesn't require me to be disruptive. In fact, being patient and thoughtful has been key to my success." That was then. It is time to add some new arrows to your quiver and show yourself to be thoughtful *and* innovative.

No one is suggesting that you develop a whole new personality so even your best friends no longer recognize you. As always, authenticity is key and your personal brand must also emanate the vitality, interest, and dynamism appropriate to your company culture and role. You may have less to adjust than you think: given your success to date you can be sure that no one thinks of you as flat, static or boring. Still, it is up to you to adjust your knowledge and brand to the times. Your behavior and reputation must encompass the accountabilities, authority, and access of your new role.

> The test of a first-rate intelligence is the ability to
> hold two opposing ideas in the mind at the same
> time and still retain the ability to function.
> *Scott Fitzgerald*

What is important is that you see the whole. Some people see disruption; others anticipate transformation. This view reflects the differences between "content out" and "context in." If you view the context as the world—the earth—the processes are an eco-system. To see the whole requires a change in conversation and a change in mindset.

Can you go with the flow?

Mihaly Csikszentmihalyi's book *Flow—The Psychology of Optimal Experience: Steps Toward Enhancing the Quality of Life* almost instantly changed how individuals view their activities and how organizational professionals' views changed. A new mindset emerged based on the idea of "flow" as a process. Before this concept of flow permeated organizational practice, I remember conducting workshops entitled "managing ambiguity." Yes, in those days we managed everything: manage change, manage people, and manage innovation. *Flow* led me to see and think differently.

> What makes an experience genuinely satisfying is a state of consciousness called flow. During flow, people typically experience deep enjoyment, creativity, and a total involvement with life.
>
> Flow also happens when a person's skills are fully involved in overcoming a challenge that is just about manageable, so it acts as a magnet for learning new skills and increasing challenges.

What does leadership look like when it flows?

Leaders who have adjusted their thinking to the new realities experience flow in their work. Joshua Boger provides one example. Josh founded

Vertex Pharmaceuticals in 1989, personally interviewing and hiring the first 400 employees, and working side by side with them. A preeminent scientist who applied chemical modeling to drug design, Josh is also an innovator, educator, philosopher and adventurer. Unlike most CEO founders, who stay in their roles past their time, Josh adjusted his sights and moved forward—he called it retirement—in 2009. He didn't just focus on his 1000 dive trip; on the contrary, the former Chairman of BIO (the biopharmaceutical industry trade association) immediately shifted his energy, enthusiasm and intellect into a number of roles that include Chairman, vice-chair, director, or member of more than a dozen medical, scientific, and not-for-profit boards. I recommend that you Google Josh—you will probably look at his list of professional activities and think, "He can't be doing all that—he is probably just on the letterhead of all those organizations!" Yes, he really *is* chairing high-level committees, continuing to find treatments for genetic diseases and much more.

Work isn't and doesn't have to be drudgery. People whose work occurs as flow do not experience "work" the way many of us do—especially on Friday afternoons. Time, talent and contribution flow together and there may not be enough hours in the day. Two other people I have personally observed work with flow are former Xerox CEO Anne Mulcahy and Judge William H. Webster, former Director of the Federal Bureau of Investigation and the Central Intelligence Agency. These leaders of very different organizations share many personal characteristics: boundless energy, athletic prowess, and insatiable curiosity. They are invigorated by conversations and always ask compelling questions; they transformed their organizations and earned the respect of their employees and constituents. Most importantly, they seemed to enjoy every moment of every day.

When asked at the Commonwealth Institute for her tips on successful leadership, Mulcahy outlined the following:

- Spend time listening—listen to customers and employees
- Communicate face to face—meet with people where they are
- Make goals clear—let employees know what is expected
- Give people a roadmap—give people a sense of hope grounded in reality
- Be honest—you must to be transparent and honest with customers and employees
- Lead and manage to values—have a clear and consistent set of values
- Challenge the status quo—make the tough calls

- Focus on things that matter—things that add value not complexity
- Inspire your people—inspire them to be and do more
- Invest upstream—cut costs and increase productivity while investing upstream

Could there be a better check list for a "context-in" mindset? One theme connects these tips: Mindset—your perspective. Focus on context and process. It is about "them," not about "you." Stay open and alert and adjust your thinking to real people, situations, current challenges and the future that is on the horizon.

Now it's your turn. What have you learned about adjusting your thinking? Add your thoughts and ideas below:

Questions	Yes/No	Actions
Given my new role, am I open to change? – *Really?*		
Have I identified the fears, concerns or challenges that "close" my thinking?		
Am I alert and aware of the impact of the context on my current role/content?		
Do I have the "right" processes in place to get me to the envisioned future?		
Do I have an engaging and inclusive communication strategy?		
Have I identified the benefits of succeeding in this role: to myself, my family, key stakeholders and to the overall organization?		
Have I identified the occasions/activities when work "flows" for me?		

13

Am I Networking Effectively?

More business decisions occur over
lunch and dinner than at any other time,
— Peter Drucker —

"You are so connected," my friends always tell me, but for years I didn't get what they were talking about because I misunderstood networking. I thought networking was an activity—something you "do"—not a relationship. Of course, I naturally stayed in touch with friends and loved bringing people from my eclectic communities together. I had strong connections with my friends and knew that they would do anything for me as I would for them. But, how ironic—I never thought to ask. I realized that I could do a better job networking.

For example, when I was selected a White House Fellow, I entered a network of relationships: People whom I viewed as friends and colleagues who shared an extraordinary experience. But I did not realize at first that my Class and the alumni network we joined could develop into a community of mutual support. Now I see my network as communities I belong to, not "meetings I have to go to."

If you are networking effectively you are building a lifetime of community, but I have learned that social status, culture and ethnicity shape our approach to networking. My friend Barbara and I often talk about networking being common *sense* but not common *practice*, especially for those who have overcome social and cultural hurdles by being rugged individuals—self starters. We were raised to do it on our own and ask for help only as a last resort. I find this mindset is particularly hard-wired into women, Latinos, African Americans and others who are culturally or ethnically outside the mainstream. To them, networking feels like an activity, not a relationship. It can be challenging to break the twin mindsets of "it takes so much work and effort" and "I wouldn't bother my friends with *that*." Sometimes my African American colleagues and I joke about missed networking opportunities and what late bloomers we are when it comes to networking effectively. One friend wryly puts it this way: "When it comes to networking, we didn't get the memo."

I have referred several times to my first executive opportunity—a time when I hunkered down to "work" behind my closed office door and avoided my colleagues, actions that led to a colossal job failure. One of the lessons I drew from this instructive but humbling experience was how valuable a strong and supportive network *would have been* to me in that situation. Many people believe that the only time to focus on building and sustaining their network is when they are seeking a new position. Don't forget that networking isn't a thing to do; a network is a place in which you orient yourself. You create and in some part inherit (e.g., alumni associations, family friends, etc.) your network of affiliations and connections, and your reputation and identify are knitted into the social fabric of your network. If you treat members of your network carefully it will blossom into a mutual support system that will always be there for you, and you for it. Networking is a full-time and life-time activity, and never more important than when you are in a key leadership role, especially a new one.

After all, one of the realities of your current role that is most different from your previous roles is the level and degree of access you now enjoy—access to power, to information, to other senior executives, to other parts of the organization. You don't take advantage of this by checking spreadsheets at your desktop; you do it by reaching out and networking.

You sharpen your networking skills every day, starting with your current group of friends and colleagues. To answer the question, "Am I networking effectively?" consider your responses to the following questions:

- Do my friends and colleagues inspire me?
- Are our conversations full of insight? Am I often surprised at the twists and turns they take?
- Does my network have a small "core" with shared values at the center?
- Do members of the network make new people feel welcome to join, while others naturally grow in other directions and move away from the group?

126

- Do network members support and help each other?
- Is my network diverse by age, ethnicity, style, profession, etc.? Do we have diverse experiences and interesting stories to share?
- Do I enjoy reaching out in all directions—up, across, and down— to expand my network?

Do you notice a pattern as you answer these questions? If you answered mostly "yes," then you have recognized that networks have energy and synergy—being in a strong network is enjoyable. Networking is personal, even intimate, and reciprocity emerges naturally within your defined group. Having a "defined group" doesn't mean you have just one group or category of friends. Networks overlap; they cross boundaries of interest and have different cadences of involvement. For a model, take a look at your social networks—Google+, LinkedIn or Facebook and notice how you grant access to some people in one venue and to different sets in others. Similarly, you have networks of friends and colleagues that overlap, and networks of colleagues and professional affiliations that seem to orbit one another, only touching because you link them together.

But what if you answered "no" to most of the questions? Let's look at why, and what you need to do to get your networking back on track.

What if I don't have time to network?

Oh please! Stop. If you don't have time to network it means that you aren't thinking about it the right way. You have put your work and your life in separate buckets and have ignored the reality: you have *one* life. Get this straight: If you are working over 60 hours per week, you do not have a bright line separating your private and business lives.

Unfortunately, networking and networking events are often viewed as add-on tasks, not only separate from work but activities that steal valuable work time or force you to trade off family time for an awkward social outing. Recognize that because you devote so many hours to your career, the boundaries between work and play have blurred, especially as it relates to who you call your "friends": college chums, friends from your former place of employment, friends who work in same company or industry, the colleagues you meet for drinks and the customers you know well—all these count as friends. With these friends, when work topics ebb in and out of the conversation during social occasions, it seems timely and appropriate.

When I ask my clients about their networks, many report only the most professional connections, especially the ones they feel they "have to" make, and omit their "friends." This suggests just how narrowly and incorrectly most people view networking.

When you think of networking as going to events, asking for favors, looking for sales, hunting for a new job, or other burdensome tasks, it quickly becomes something you don't have time for! Instead, replace the word *networking* with *connecting, collaborating, partnering, socializing* or *staying in touch*. Now do you have time? Of course you do. Think about your work colleagues with whom you have a solid relationship (maybe even a friendship). Or if you prefer, begin with professional associates external to your organization. List one or two names in each category. Do not include people you do not like.

Category for Connecting	Colleagues
We have a tight connection	
I collaborate with	
We partnered on …	
My spouse/partner socialize	
After work, we	
I can count on	
On weekends we	
Our kids or spouses …	

Additional categories: _____

_____

_____

Why do you need to refresh your network?

My friend Susie, an avid gardener, describes networking as organic: Her advice is plant the seeds, make certain the soil is fertile (mutuality), provide the nourishment and weather the sun and the rain (good times and bad). Remember that as plants grow they expand, so from time to time you will need to prune your network so that you can grow. If necessary, pull out the weeds (any members of your network whom you no longer trust, for example). The result will be a network that is like a beautiful garden—and the harvest is the collective talents, connections and wisdom of all its members.

If you view your network as organic and living, you know that it requires attention or, to continue the gardening theme, it requires tending. How will you know when it's time to tend your network? One sign is when the circle seems too small. It is natural to grow apart from some people as your lives and careers take different paths. Or you may notice that you avoid spending time with some members. When relationships grow stale, you feel stuck in the past or bored, or you find yourself slipping into old habits you would rather drop, just to maintain a friendship. When it seems that you are simply repeating activities and conversations—without much joyfulness—it's time to refresh your network, and the best way to refresh your network is by expanding it, adding new members. Don't eliminate people from your network, unless you plan to move far, far away. These people will be part of your "circle" even if you don't see them as often; don't make an enemy or cut off a relationship that might improve in the future.

I follow these three guidelines:

1 I surround myself with friends who lift me higher,
2 I am present and engaged when I am with them; and
3 We have absorbing conversations that avoid negativity and gossip.

And, sometimes, we just sit and watch the sunset at Menemsha Beach. I have learned that the quality of your life is determined by the quality of the conversations you engage in. You know that it is time to refresh your network if the conversations are full of whining and complaints, or it it's predicable that as soon as you sit down with some people the same topic comes up, the same words pour out and the energy (and in some cases the relationship) is sucked out of the room.

Granted, I have a few "curmudgeon" members of my network who fit this description, yet they remain in my network. It is a conscious choice I have made. When the predicable whining and complaining begin, it's up to me to change the topic to a more positive and energetic one. You may be thinking, "That's rude, I wouldn't just change the subject!" Think again; you can change a conversation without being rude, condescending, or uncaring. My approach is to be authentic and compassionate, and find an early opening to introduce a new subject. One way is to get the person off the couch and into a shared activity. You won't take this approach with everyone; but you probably already give some members of your network a lot

---

C-Suite Mindset

YOUR PEERS AND BOSS ARE IN YOUR NETWORK

Advisor: Carolyn Chin
CEO, Cebiz a Consulting Investing firm, and Co-founder of
"OnBoard Bootcamps," seminars for those seeking to join boards

Of course you want to be positively branded; you want the reputation for being a superstar in a certain area. You also must have a reputation for being very good with your team. But this is most important: Cover your boss—don't embarrass your boss. Don't make your boss look stupid, ever!

If I did anything differently to network more effectively it would be get peer support. I was able to "stay there" because I had the top support and the troops behind me, which is the way that you get systemic change. Peer support would have strengthened my hand even more.

---

of rope in this area. The longstanding friendship is important to you, and you recognize that your friend is just in a funk or a rut, or going through a challenging time. In other words, it is a phase and not a destination. If your friend has reached his or her destination, a lack of shared interests will usually cause you to drift apart.

> Your network of friends, colleagues, clients
> and customers is the most important marketing
> tool you've got; what they say about you and your
> contributions is what the market will ultimately
> gauge as the value of your brand.
> *Tom Peters*

Where will I find interesting people?

Because networks evolve and people come and go, I recommend that you consciously "refresh" your network. For example, until recently, I may have been one of the few women in America who wasn't in a book club. I accepted the invitation to join the Boston Book Club because I wanted to meet new people; specifically, I wanted to meet interesting people with whom I don't have a professional affiliation. The women in my book club include long time New Englanders and new arrivals; their backgrounds include academics, technology, biotechnology, social work and hospitality. I have gained refreshing new perspectives and insights, not to mention connections into several new "tangent" networks. I also added an Isabella Stewart Gardner Museum concert series to my calendar with the dual aim of enjoying beautiful music and creating serendipitous opportunities to make new friends. And, my new board affiliation with the Boston Museum of Science provides endless opportunities to learn and grow. Making your "refreshment" activity one you really enjoy will not only get you out the door to the events, it will assure that the conversations you have are authentic and meaningful.

When you are curious about people and their ideas, networking becomes a way to reach into new communities of ideas. Consider the quality of your life—yes, both personal and professional—and answer this: What conversations would be enriching?

- Having a dialogue with industry/organizational thought leaders
- Discussing how to operate as a power couple
- Discussing nannies and schooling
- Exploring …
- Exchanging ideas about….
- Mentoring…
- Contributing…
- Challenging current thinking
- Learning
- Debating…

Once you have identified the one or two categories of conversation that intrigue you—for example, meeting thought leaders in nanotechnology and exchanging ideas about future trends—you can develop a list of the current members in your network who may be separated by one or two degrees from people in these fields. Then invite someone to lunch!

People that you don't know but would like to meet.	• •
Member of my network who knows them.	• •
Member of my network knows someone who knows them.	• •

Occasionally you hear of networking raised almost to an art form. Effective networking can even make the news, as this bit from the *New York Times* shows:

> How did this young woman, with no special family or literary connections, manage to wrangle some big names around the unlikeliest of projects—a monthly literary magazine?
>
> The answer is that Ms. Maduka, or Max to her friends, has combined an unusual charisma with sheer determination to meet the right people, find the right parties and propel herself into the city's literary set.

How will expanding my network help me improve?

I have a client who is very skillful at determining how to keep his network fresh and then taking the initiative to reach out and build his network. The steps he takes are simple:

1 Initiate or follow up with a person of interest, admiration or curiosity.

2 Be present and engaged; make a connection in a shared area of interest or significance (note *significance* means *importance to you*, not *dour* or *serious*).

For example, Maurice recounted his first meeting with the CEO of a large firm.

> When Oliver and I met, we talked about leadership and his personal life style. One topic flowed into another and I asked him how he got his beliefs about the value of a diverse workforce to his firm's global strategy. His answer went far beyond marketing. As a result, I learned that you have to give people a break. Let them make mistakes, take risks, prove themselves. Oliver believes that with the right attitude and environment everyone can succeed.
>
> Oliver is also very connected. He meets with the CEOs of half a dozen major companies monthly for dinner. It's sort of a kitchen cabinet or in some instances a team of rivals.
>
> It was a great first meeting. I plan to stay in touch. We definitely connected.

After this meeting, Maurice continued to follow up with people who captured his interest and attention. He also reached out to possible mentors (see Chapter 4) advocates and allies. His networking was effective because it became the way that he conducted his business, reached out to clients and stayed intellectually stimulated. Yes, networking was organic for Maurice.

How often should you meet?

"K.I.S.S." You have a lot of ways to keep the conversation going and grow your friendship. You don't need to schedule a luncheon every time you meet. Accept an offer to drop by the office or connect when in town; send emails or Skype for birthdays and promotions, when a noteworthy event takes place or article is published. Attend a basketball game, play a round of golf, go for a run or take a yoga class if these are interests you share. Remember: invite and engage. Generously extend invitations and when you meet make it a fun and engaging conversation.

Clients often ask me, "How often should I reach out to or meet members of my network?" There is no right or wrong answer because the frequency or cadence of each relationship varies. It can be daily, weekly, monthly; we all have the person we may not see for months—even years—yet when we do connect it is as if we had never been separated. The appropriate timing will be obvious if you are attentive to the flow of energy or synergy in your conversations. If you think, "WOW that was great—let's meet and invite so-and-so to join us too!" then schedule a date. Or, if one or both of you are introverts your meeting might end more quietly and you might need time to think about the conversation. You might feel better following up via email and meeting quarterly.

If it is a business contact, always be respectful of their time. The more seniority the person has (or the more levels there are between you), the more time you should allow to elapse between in-person meetings—maybe 4-6 months if the person is very senior and, if the person is in Dubai, you may meet once a year. If you are both committed to the connection and there is a spark of friendship that can flame, be authentic and creative and keep the conversation going back and forth.

The more you network, the more people you will meet. You might even meet someone and just "click"—you already share some of the same friends and interests and you work or live in close proximity. You are excited when you meet and the relationship just takes off. You may even start to think about business deals you can pursue. This person may be a new addition to your core network—one you wouldn't have discovered if you hadn't reached out.

What if you don't have any real friends at work?

If you are in a place where you don't have friends, I hope that you are looking for a new job because you are in a toxic, stressful environment. Bottom line, you wouldn't be reading this chapter if you had no friends at work!

A more relevant question is, "What is a real friend at work?" The answer can be found in Chapter 3. Your colleagues offer you remarkable breadth and depth of experience. Individually, they are your "go-to people" for organizational information and know-how. Your current circle is likely to be one person removed from the resources or information that you need. As a result of this proximity, you will have *access*; you will be able to use your influence to get things done. Once mobilized, these connections will accelerate your ability to get your arms around the scope of any task. Because your trusted friends and allies have your back, you can step out of your comfort zone with confidence.

Just remember to differentiate between true friends and business acquaintances and, as always, use your common sense when discussing tough or personal issues if your work colleagues don't spill over into other areas of your life. If you have drawn the boundary around some conversations, you have probably made a decision about trust—bottom line: they aren't real friends. Stick to a more formal and less open relationship.

Your goal is to make networking effortless and fluid: your friends, spouse or partner, colleagues, professional colleagues, contacts, and clients all belong to your network. Your network reaches vertically both up and down, and spans horizontally within your organization's walls and beyond.

Final note: I have discovered that almost everyone can take their networking to a higher level and that the changing dynamics of today demand that we do. Check out one of my favorite books about networking, *Never Eat Alone* by Keith Ferrazzi (the book with the bright orange cover that already may be sitting on your bookshelf!).

Ferrazzi makes it clear by his own life example that a network is a circle of relationships forged over a lifetime of meaningful interactions. The value of the advice in this book in summed up in the descriptive line on the cover: How to build a lifelong community of colleagues, contacts, friends and mentors.

Never Eat Alone: And Other Secrets to Success, One Relationship at a Time. Read it.

Now it's your turn. What actions will you take to make your networking more effective? Add your thoughts and ideas below:

	Questions	Yes/No	Actions
ALERT?	• Have I made a visual or hard copy network map? • Do I understand and appreciate the role of each member of my network (inform, inspire etc.)?		
ADJUST?	• Do I understand the gaps in my network? • Am I aware of the key people (and networks) that can effect my success in this role?		
ALIGN?	• Am I weeding, watering and planting new seeds? • Am I reactivating relevant former networks?		
ACT?	• Am I reaching out, up and across? • Do I appreciate and understand the benefit of my charitable or social activities?		

Here is what your action plan might look like:

Action	Rationale
I will draw a network map	• Visualize and make certain it includes friends
I will identify the members of my network that enrich and inspire me	• Nurture my network; spend time with these members
I will identify the separate groups that make up my network	• Analyze value and benefit, as well as frequency of contact
Weed or prune	• Be clear that people that I don't like are not in my close network
Invigorate a member of network	• Help get a longstanding friend out of a rut
Add new members	• Add spice to my life—engage in new conversations

14

How Can I Stay Open to Change?

Where there is an open mind, there will always be a frontier.
— Charles F. Kettering —

Hannah was at the top of her game. After leading the most success-ful product development effort in her company's history, she had been rewarded three years ago with a VP role. Things were going well at home, too. Her youngest child was a high school junior and her hus-band had just gotten university tenure when her boss took her aside.

> Honestly, it was the last thing I expected! An offer to head up the London office. Five years ago I would have killed for that, but now....? I had to really examine myself and my motiva-tions—do I want to continue to grow in this organization? Can I juggle all the complexity of my life and add this too? Isn't it time to dial it back a little?

Continuing up the spiral career ladder, Hannah has earned the right to "kick back" because of the ease and flow with which she wields her subject matter expertise. Hannah discovered that staying there almost always comes with an opportunity to get somewhere new, which means being open to change.

Do you think things are fine just as they are?

Maybe you are thinking, "Life is good! I wish I could do a freeze frame right now!" And, maybe you should stay put for now especially if every member of your family seems satisfied. But change is swirling around you all the time, in every aspect of life—your family, your company, your industry, technology, and the larger world of politics and econom-ics and for you—change is calling you forward. Or, you may be at the other end of the scale: you've managed to insulate yourself from some of the change. Maybe you've streamlined your life and can coast on your routines. But then, just when everything seems to be going along nicely, *wham!* And unless you are ready to pack it in, you need to be open to change in all its forms.

Do you have a good routine, or are you stuck in a rut?

It may seem ironic that you must always challenge the very routines that help you lead your life efficiently, but the more you have settled into a comfortable routine, the more likely it is that you are stuck in a rut. The fact is, recent research shows us that even if you are happy with the status quo, you need new experiences to keep your brain functioning at its peak. From the perspective of neuroscience, change and learning are the same thing. They are what keep us open to more change rather than settling for an ever-narrowing circle of experiences. They are what prepare us to welcome exciting new assignments instead of being a good citizen and marking time in a corporate backwater.

Maybe you look happy and successful and nobody except you knows you are stuck. You wonder, "What happened? Did I drive off the side of the road?" In the middle of a successful career, few people are content to say, "I'm stuck and happy about that. I'll stay here and that's good news." When you notice that you are in a rut, you are more likely asking, "How do I get out of here?!"

C-Suite Mindset

DON'T BECOME A GOOD CITIZEN

Advisor: Douglas Marshall
Business Strategist

In a large corporation, you can become a part of the frozen middle—it permits you to make some kind of contribution and pick up the salary check. You can become a good citizen and good citizens don't get fired. Many people retire in their jobs and can't imagine themselves doing other things. You have to position yourself like a trapeze artist to grab the next opportunity. As for me, being satisfied in my work is the greatest reward.

Or you might challenge me and say, "Not me! I am not in a rut; I do something different every day. We have the latest technology, our customers give us the highest rating and our profitability shows in our stock price." OK. If you are not in a rut, what is the latest book you read? Tell me about your most recent trip? What are you learning from your research project? What are you doing to improve your golf swing or your tennis game? What are you learning from your children?

It's hard to be truly open to change in some areas of your life while you rest in a rut in others. The habit of complacency has an unfortunate tendency to spill over. This is not to say you can't enjoy respite and comfort in your life, or dive into a big bowl of mac and cheese after a hard day. There is a difference between intentionally relaxing and coasting. It's fine to kick back for a while, but if you want to be ready for and welcome the next big thing, you need to embrace learning and change. The good news is, people who have experienced a variety of different situations tend to react better to change than those with narrower experiences. You may be surprised to notice that your younger colleagues have more trouble handling change than you do!

How can you climb out of your rut?

If you are in a rut, the important thing is to climb out. Being open to change takes practice. Leaving well-worn paths behind, even in matters as small as the route you take to the office or the sports you play, stimulates your brain and makes it work. Like any other ability, "use it or lose it!" Exercising your "change muscles" will increase your mental and physical agility. How can you keep flexing this change muscle? Start by incorporating one of these practices into your life.

- Begin a mindful or restorative practice. Take up meditation, yoga or even napping.
- Move your body. Take the stairs, walk instead of driving everywhere. Get a pedometer and discover how easy it is to cover 10,000 steps a day. Research indicates that exercise is good for the brain.
- Enjoy the beauty that surrounds you. Position your desk so that you can look out a window; visit a museum; track the stars each week on skyandtelescope.com.
- Explore. Each day, make a point of doing something you wouldn't ordinarily do. Sit and enjoy your coffee at Starbucks instead of taking it out; make a telephone call when an email would "do"; travel; learn a new skill or language.

- Socialize. Build and enjoy multiple networks of friends. You'll be stimulated by their conversations and open to diverse points of view.

If none of these activities grabs your interest, find one that does. Take up a new sport, hobby, or musical instrument. Take a class or attend a conference. Move your body and stretch your mind. In my own case, one new practice—taking up the sport of cycling—has shown me how pushing myself in one area permeates all aspects of my life. Cycling gives me adventure, open space, and beautiful vistas. Intense physical activity gets me out of the box of cerebral work. Mastering and excelling in a sport keeps me open to change and gives me more staying power—what will I try next? With every ride, I am traveling a new road: seeing a turtle sunning on a rock or taking pleasure in catching fellow cyclists on a hill and blowing past them. In bicycling I compete against myself. I tested my endurance by riding 300 miles in three days (Boston to New York, averaging 18 mph) and later riding almost 500 miles in six days, going from Minneapolis to Chicago at a faster pace. Who knows what goals I'll set and achieve next?

Do you seek out new experiences?
If not, what's your excuse?

Most people answer that second question with one word: *time.* Who has the time to take up a new activity or do something new? The answer is that *no one does,* until they realize the value of making it a priority. How do you make time for the priorities in your life—the weekly meeting with your boss or the annual check-up with your doctor? You allot the time and create a space—literally create an opening. In other words, you stop what you are doing; I call it "pressing the pause button."

Press the pause button to make space for new experiences. Run this simple experiment: keep 15 to 30 minutes "blank" during the course of your day, every day, and see what happens. Make a commitment to keep the "blank" time slot open. Don't fill it with last minute calls or meetings. As Peter Drucker advises:

> Follow effective action with quiet reflection. From the quiet reflection will come even more effective action.

Being open to change doesn't happen at the end of your to-do list or when you finally have free time. Being open happens by design. You have to create your own supportive environment and the first step is carving out a blank space in your schedule for reflection—or "thought-ful review."

Next, actually use the space to welcome new experiences. Shift your focus from problem solving to reflection. Close your door and open a space for introspection. Don't worry if you don't solve the world's problems in your first fifteen minutes. And don't rush through your blank time so you can "get back to work" or use it to plan your next presentation. Instead, adopt an attitude of *luxuriating* in your free time. Indulge yourself: Spending time thinking, reflecting and generat-ing new ideas is good for your brain. When my friend Maia made a career change, "luxuriating" helped her find a new business model:

> I really took my time. I socialized with friends, traveled to new and exotic places. I met new people and had dozens of con-versations on all kinds of topics, many of them not even related to my main quest. But it all paid off handsomely; the insights I gleaned gave me first-mover advantage when I made my play. In the end I built a million-dollar business in the home health care market. I would never come to this if I hadn't taken that pause.

Start with small things: capture your good ideas that are relevant to a future conversation; think about your goals for the week. Move on to using the time to focus on your thoughts, accomplishments and dreams. You will know that your time is well spent when "just thinking" leaves you energized or smiling.

Earl Walker, VP for Client Services pressed the pause button and used the space to reflect on his areas of growth.

> What have I been doing the last couple of months? I have been in this role for three years now. What is different now? Plenty! Reflecting on my goals and compiling my accomplishments builds my confidence; it makes me comfortable to say what I believe and let people judge me for that.
>
> We are preparing for the last quarter—we are getting into promotions and I am in the running for a big one this year. I have taken a step back and now see what it means to be Earl Walker. I see that I add a lot of value. I understand my position in the dynamic of the organization and I have taken the time to map out the different relationships that I need to forge both in the short term and, more to the point, that I will need to forge

to succeed in the new role I aspire to. Taking the time to really think about these things puts everything in focus. I see that I can either row my boat in the direction I want to go, or just be swept along in the firm's changes. I'd rather row.

> The purpose of life is to live it, to taste experience
> to the utmost, to reach out eagerly and without fear
> for newer and richer experience.
> *Eleanor Roosevelt*

How do you plan to increase your staying power?

One way to develop your capacity to change is by exploring your nascent or heretofore latent talents. In my coaching practice, I have noticed that most people shut down a part of themselves because they are convinced they just "don't have time." Pressing the pause button will show you that you do have time for the things you make important. "Indulging yourself" in an interest, a passion, or an activity yields wide-ranging benefits. Being curious and actively engaged is key, not just to staying current in this fast moving global environment, but also to your self-confidence and sense of value. New experiences give you a fresh perspective and whet your appetite for more adventures. Accepting the risk of putting paint on canvas or fingers on frets will embolden you in ways you would not imagine. For example, Chris decided to take up a musical instrument:

> I want to have a fuller life, a great life. I am playing the violin.
> It's something I've always wanted to do. It wasn't easy to start—
> it sounded awful! But I kept at it, and I've learned a lot about
> myself in the process.

Taking up the violin is just the visible (or audible!) result of Chris's decision to step back, embrace something new, risk failure, and persevere. Not surprisingly, she saw the benefits of her efforts spill over into other facets of her life and found herself spreading her wings in other areas.

> After I started violin lessons, I was invited to be on the engineer-
> ing council. In the past I would have accepted, of course, but I
> would have second-guessed my competence and taken a back
> seat. I took a leadership role in the women's council and gained
> visibility as speaker. Then I found the courage to ask my boss to

advocate for my early promotion to director. I know all this isn't just from playing the violin—I think it's because I am more willing to stretch toward new challenges.

Does your environment support exploration and change?

Look around. Are the people in your immediate environment—your friends, family and colleagues—open to change? Are they stimulating and interesting? Do they relate to change with "Bring it on!" or with suspicion or fear? If the people close to you avoid change they probably don't want you to change either. They expect you to be reliable and predicable—to remain basically the same. If your personal brand is as solid as concrete, changing now could be as risky as replacing the "old" Coca-cola with the "new" Coke. If you suggest moving in a new direction, you might hear comments like, "You've made it, don't stress yourself now;" "Relax—you've earned it;" "Why would you want to take that on at your age?" or "You might not be successful at that" and "I did that and I didn't like it."

Don't be caught in these spider webs of complacency! Approach your escape from your rut strategically and nimbly. Remember the four inevitable downsides of change (see Chapter 5) and consider how they will affect your personal and professional stakeholders. Then, my advice is to remember the management principal of "no surprises" and bring your stakeholders along with you on your new path.

1 Declare a change in your pattern. Let them know that you are on a new path or at new stage of growth.

2 Convey your emotion. "I am excited/enthusiastic/curious/intrigued." Make it sound like an adventure and exploration.

3 Describe the benefit. "This is something that I always wanted to do" or "I am glad to be painting/ playing the piano again" or "This new role will put me right in the action—it will be exciting to shape the next phase."

Don't be deterred if some of your friends or colleagues like you just the way you are. You are exploring new areas of personal and professional growth and you don't need their approval. Over time your new interest and insights will lead you to a wider circle or even a new circle of like-minded people. Enjoy!

- Do something different each day

- Do something for yourself
- Reward yourself
- See the beauty all around you
- Look up—enjoy the blue sky and the stars

If you deliberately alter your routine, you open yourself to a world of new possibilities. For example, when I began coaching Jeff he described his "problem" as time management. He said, "I realize that I juggle too many things at one time; things fall through the cracks." I asked a few questions about the quality of his life: It was all work and very little play. I advised him to pause and try something new. Six weeks later he was brimming with excitement and, to my surprise, he said:

> I brought a bike and I am going to do a triathlon! I haven't been swimming since high school and I hired a swim coach. I plan to ride a 1000 miles and I am now at 600. I have discovered a whole network of eclectic people involved in triathlons. The triathlon types are very world-smart and they come from dozens of different firms and institutions. It makes networking easy.

You may be wondering, what did Hannah—the client profiled at the beginning of this chapter—choose? After much thought and many conversations with her family, Hannah decided to accept the London opportunity for a two-year stint, with her family staying at home and generous travel arrangements. A big change, and she embraced it.

Dr. Seuss's last book, is a great send-off into life's adventures, challenges, and changes. It celebrates the success of *you*, with "brains in your head" and "feet in your shoes." Using your brains and your feet, you can choose wisely and react nimbly to the changes before you. Embrace change! You don't want to end up in "The Waiting Place,"

...for people just waiting.
Waiting for a train to go
or a bus to come, or a plane to go
or the mail to come, or the rain to go
or the phone to ring, or the snow to snow
or waiting around for a Yes or a No
or waiting for their hair to grow.
Everyone is just waiting.

Now it's your turn. What will you do to stay open to new experiences? Add your thoughts and ideas below:

		Questions	Yes/No	Actions
ALERT?		• Am I in a rut? By choice or by default? • Am I able to grow in place? • Am I ready to go?		
ADJUST?		• Am I interested in new opportunities? • Willing to close any gaps in skill, knowledge, style? • Do I have a plan that works for me and my key stakeholders?		
ALIGN?		• Does my network encourage personal and professional growth? • Does my next step naturally "flow"? • Is my next step a major change in direction?		
ACT?		• Am I "happy" with the steps/choices made at this point in my career? • Have I made changes to my calendar/schedule? • Do I include fresh and novel activities? • Have I added new members to my network?		

15

How Do I Use My Access, Power, and Influence?

*The most common way people give away their power
is by thinking they don't have any.*

— Alice Walker —

Recently promoted to Senior Vice President, Stanley had big plans that would revolutionize his division.

> Moving to an inventory-less system will touch every job—from factory floor to sales to customer service. I can implement this in some areas directly, and Evelyn over in Sales is with me. But I can't seem to get Phil on board with the idea. He has the smallest piece of the puzzle, but he's slowing everything down. And he definitely has the CEO's ear. Things seem to work differently up here on the fourth floor—it's not enough to just have a good idea.

The farther you advance in your career, the more important and valuable will be the interplay between access, power, and influence. Even though you are "in charge" of more people than ever before, your actual authority over others is not what determines your ability to set the tone, define the game, and achieve your desired outcomes. Staying there is a result of how you use the power, influence, and access your position entails. In the scenario above, Stanley should take a lesson from Phil, who seems to have taken full advantage of his influence and access.

What is influence?

Influence is the ability to get what we want without compelling people to do what we say. Specifically, it is a way to extend your reach. Through influence, we can affect outcomes beyond the reach of our authority. Don't dismiss being influential as just manipulating people. Influence is earned—it is based on competence, credibility, and confidence. When Stanley considered Phil, he quickly identified one obvious source of his influence.

> Phil has been with the firm fifteen years. He worked his way up and knows the place inside and out.

For his part, Stanley also brings something to the table. The expertise supporting his proposal was one of the major factors behind his promotion to General Manager. His strong track record has earned him the respect of the CEO and members of the board. But he is still operating as if he were in his former role. Stanley needs to seize the power, access, and influence now at his disposal. Which of your colleagues are most influential with their peers and superiors? What can you learn from them?

What is power?

Dictionaries define power as the ability to do something, to act, or produce an effect. While it is based on your actual organizational or hierarchical authority, your power extends far beyond your spot on the organizational chart. It is the sum of your authority, status, rank, and the skills and expertise you offer—your competence, credibility, and confidence.

Like other components of success, your power is what you make of it and is very susceptible to being drained away by thoughtless actions. Consider: when you pass your boss in the hallway and she asks, "How's it going?" what do you say? If you simply answer "Fine" you have just thrown away your power. Likewise, if you sit through a meeting without contributing, or if you speak so softly that no one can hear you, you are throwing your power away. Power is a muscle, and the way to strengthen it is by flexing it.

> Power is like being a lady.
> If you have to tell people you are, you aren't.
> *Margaret Thatcher*

What does "access" mean in your role?

It's not what you know, but how quickly you are known and accepted. With every new position, you enter a new circle of peers, and your sphere of contacts rises accordingly. Access means more than the ability to get on someone's calendar. Who do you eat lunch with? Whose office do you drop into for coffee and informal conversation? Casual and often unscheduled meetings are the benefits of access at the senior level. Remember, throughout your career, you are usually one step removed from the resources you need. At your level, using your access brings many more resources to bear on your projects.

It's easy to underestimate the shift in the power/influence/access dynamic when you take on a new role. A few times in my own past, I squandered an opportunity to fully utilize my access, influence and power in new roles and situations. I tripped over several common pitfalls:

- I did not appreciate the level of power, influence and access that were at my disposal
- When I asked for something, I didn't ask for enough, and
- I stumbled over the moment where I had the greatest leverage.

Each time, the outcome would have been a whole lot better if I had been prepared.

Access, power and influence are dynamically interconnected. In Chapter 8 you learned the "use it or lose it" rule: if you don't use your access, influence and power you lose them. Yet if you do use them properly, each serves as a multiplier for the others. Taking advantage of your access creates more occasions to be influential and as a result more opportunities to be powerful. In turn, you empower others by granting them access—meeting with them—and taking action on their good ideas. This critical and sometimes neglected part of the cycle is paying it forward: anyone who stays there realizes that today's direct report today could be tomorrow's colleague or boss.

With the mutually reinforcing nature of influence, access, and power in mind, it is time to recalibrate the people in your network and take stock of your expectations (see Chapters 3 and 9) and current role. Review and recalibrate by considering the following aspects of your current reality. Note: be specific and include all categories that apply.

1 I now have access to .....
2 I have opportunities to influence
  - Decisions...
  - Strategy...
  - Finances ...
  - Resources...

- Innovation ...
- Clients/Markets/Products...

3 The power (status) implicit in this new role
  - The *explicit* power/status
  - My scope of influence
  - The tangibles and intangibles that I bring to the table
  - My impact

What is different about your situation now from the past? Have you considered how your changes in power, influence, and access will affect your ability to perform? Have you examined how the opportunities interweave and connect—for example, Stanley can use his increased access to the CEO to find more opportunities to work directly with Phil and build a deeper level of trust with him. He might use his influence with major clients to enlist them as advocates for some of the changes he is proposing. To fully settle into your role, be clear about W.I.I.F.M.—remember that identifying the benefit to you is not a selfish act. On the contrary, you are aligning your values and aspirations; by asking, you gain clarity and are grounded. If you are new in your role, answer the following questions:

1 What is the benefit to me of accepting this new role?
2 How does it benefit my boss? Colleagues? Other key stakeholders?
3 How will I use my access?
4 What are the areas that I can influence?
5 What implicit and explicit power does this new role convey?
6 Where are my opportunities to empower others?
7 Who do I need to add to my network?
8 What style or behavioral changes will make me a better leader? A better person?
9 What is my brand/reputation now?

What is different about the terrain?

You have staying power: you have a track record of growth and successfully transitioning into new roles and accountabilities. You know—perhaps from your own experience—that a mistake or misstep in this terrain can cause you to career sideways or off the cliff. Unsure about "how things work on the fourth floor," Stanley is understandably anxious. What if he does the wrong thing—steps on somebody's toes and misses his chance? It's only natural to have butterflies in your stomach when you take on a new role and move into new terrain. Of course you wonder how to get on the right track and what moves to make and when. A few butterflies are OK—but think how much less anxious you are now compared to when you were "getting there." Then, without experience and skills, you worried about whether you even had access, could be influential, or had any real power. Unlike then, you are not stopped in your tracks now—you are getting the right footing to traverse the terrain. As always, be alert, look up and around; listen for cues and consider how the view is different from this vantage point.

After all, you have arrived at this stage because you have utilized your access, influence and power effectively so far. Your goal is to step into your role with confidence—seeing yourself with the same lens as your boss, colleagues, clients and board members. Here's what others see when the look at you in your new role:

Your role	How others see you
Are you new as an individual contributor?	• Your specialized expertise, know-how or leadership will open doors for you. • Or, you are in a developmental opportunity with the visibility—senior leaders will be watching to see how effectively you navigate the role.
Are you new as a team leader?	• Respected by colleagues and management, you have demonstrated an ability to delegate, lead, and develop others. • Viewed as a team player, you will leverage your access and influence by collaborating and empowering others.
Are you a new chief of staff?	• Organizational and analytical skills are the core of your personal brand. You consistently pay attention at the "right" level of detail and/or decision-making. • You are diplomatic and maintain confidences. Your clear communications accelerate the smooth operation of projects and processes. • Your pivotal position gives you the visibility to solidify relationships with seniors while gaining a new line of sight on the competitive pressures

Your role	How others see you
Are you new to an organization (business unit, department...)?	• You work well with people and inspire them. • Your strategic thinking, product knowledge, ability to cross-sell or work across boundaries is valued by your new organization. • You see opportunities, encourage knowledge transfer and implement process improvements. • You are seen as a leader and a team player, and your pursuit of excellence is a standard for others.
Do you have a new boss?	• You complement or round out your new manager's skills or bring the skills needed to move the organization to the next level. • You have a lot of political capital with your new boss because he or she went to bat to hire you. Or you have a new boss due to an organizational change and, again, the boss decided to keep you as a member of the team • You use your "newness" to establish the best cadence of communications; you demonstrate your value early on. You earn your manager's confidence by keeping your word and not over-reaching.
Other....	

When should I use my access and ability to influence?

Seeing yourself through the eyes of others shows you that you have earned your power, influence, and access. But when and how should you exercise them? As always, be mindful of the context and the cues. Timing is everything when it comes to utilizing your access, influence or power; you need to be attuned and ask: given the current situation, the context—what is appropriate? If your organization is growing, then opportunities are everywhere. If you are in a shrinking market or your organization is cutting costs, you may not want to spend your political capital on a losing cause. But just because purse strings are tight doesn't mean you should put your plans aside. You are where you are today because you don't go underground in times of change, hibernating while awaiting better times. Use your business acumen and organiza-

tional savvy to anticipate change and position yourself for the future by
determining:

- Is now a good time to suggest/recommend?
- Is the time right to meet with...?
- Should the goal of our next step be iterative or a breakthrough?

When successfully done, you will find yourself in the right place,
with the right know-how, at the right time.

Don't make the mistake of thinking that using your access and
influence during changing times is playing politics. Positive political skills are the cornerstone of staying there. Negative politics reflect
manipulation, deception and zero-sum thinking. Positive political skills
bring the breadth, depth and relevancy of your network to the fore.
The members of your network are tuned in to the context and processes of your organization; your connections allow you to anticipate
and discuss changes coming down the pike. The bottom line is that you
are engaged and present: mindful. You notice dynamics. This is politics
at its best.

What if my style is "wait and see"?

Just because you aren't promoting a big initiative at the moment doesn't
mean you aren't utilizing power, access, and influence. "Wait and see"
doesn't mean that you are detached and inactive. And your wait-and-see
staying power brand means that others view you as rock solid, delibera-
tive or consistent. "Rock solid" does not mean immovable or inflexible.
Your colleagues know that when you throw your influence and power
behind a proposed new direction you have thoroughly questioned and
vetted the change. You have influence because your boss and colleagues
view your questions as instructive; your questions open new territory
or point to a gap in logic. Always a team player, you push back when
appropriate. Your colleagues and boss may look to you to play a key
role in the path forward because you are attentive to the process and
execution. Because of your reputation as a person who speaks softly and
sparingly, when you do speak up your words have clout.

What if I can't influence the direction?

If your timing is out of sync with the rest of your team, doors and
ears will close. People will work around you and you will probably ask
yourself: Is this a place where I want to be? Staying there doesn't mean
staying forever like Bartleby the Scrivener; you stay because you are a

valued contributor. If you find yourself in a role where everyone else is in agreement and pleased with the current direction and your questions have become a bother to them—in short, if you feel like a pariah—then it's time to move. Yes, it is up to you to figure this out. If you are out of sync at this point in your career it is likely that you have strong views that are not aligned with the company. If you are reporting to someone (including the board of directors) and find yourself at the peak or a promontory, it's time to find a new mountain to scale.

What are the things that I shouldn't do?

It may seem obvious, but remember to focus on your style and approach. *How* you use your access, influence and power is important to your staying power. For example, here are a couple of sure-fire ways to lose influence:

- Promoting yourself and upstaging others
- Making excuses for failure
- Failing to communicate
- Bad mouthing your boss

It's easy to fall back into old habits, and no one may call you on it once you get to certain levels. Check to see if you are stepping on or over people or acting like a bull in a china shop. Don't be a know-it-all. I often tell my clients that if they are the smartest person in the room they just won the booby prize. Be sure that you have impeccable integrity and are widely respected and liked. Be careful when your boss ask you to "give her feedback" on her performance or to "frankly" tell him about a co-worker's performance. (Note that I am not referring to providing feedback for the performance management process.) If you are alert, you may recognize that when you answer the question, it will press the lever to a trap door, especially if you don't have an outstanding and trusting relationship with your boss. And, if you are thinking, "You can't handle the truth," then please, please, please don't open your mouth.

Being authentic, inclusive, engaging—just being present—will give you staying power. Again, look around, up and down: who are your admirers? Followers? Collaborators? Advocates? You are known by the company you keep, and your network contributes to your personal brand. We have all seen how out of touch and ineffective people become when they are surrounded by "'yes' men and women." The bottom line: continue to be self-aware, connected and engaged.

C-Suite Mindset

WHEN IT'S NOT WORKING, MOVE ON

Advisor: Shelley Stewart, Jr.
VP & Chief Procurement Officer and Chair of Board,
Howard Business School

You have to know when it isn't working. Even if you do your homework, you don't really know how it really works until you are inside—that's when you learn the culture. You can be having fun on the job and know it's not the right "fit" for you. You have to be self-confident and know your comfort zone and your "uncomfort" zone. You have to do your due diligence and even then you may not know. It's up to you to be agile in your mind and willing to take risks.

You may also want to consider being grateful for what you have accomplished and being generous with your time, talent and treasure. These qualities are part of paying it forward, one of the foundations of staying power. In that vein, I have seen several people attain positions in business and government where they could grant access to others, but they pulled the ladder up instead of putting a hand out. How you manage the shift from seeking access to granting access has a way of establishing a tone for the future—when you might be on the other side of the door!

In summary, your facility in managing the dynamic of access, influence and power determines your staying power. People who stay there are adept at leveraging access and influence and sharing their power through collaboration and partnering. They build networks characterized by ease and reciprocity, allowing them to anticipate, engage and accomplish new tasks and challenges.

Now it's your turn. What new insights do you have and what actions will you take to use your new access, influence and power? What do you need to stop? Start? And continue?

Stop: _____

Start: _____

Continue: _____

16

How Can I Take
My Organization to
the Next Level?

A lot of companies have chosen to downsize,
and maybe that was the right thing for them.
We chose a different path. Our belief was that
if we kept putting great products in front of customers,
they would continue to open their wallets.

— Steve Jobs —

What is the best way to take your organization to the next level? Of course, there isn't a one-size-fits-all answer; it "all depends" on your competitive environment, changes in technology that drive or affect your customers' behavior, your compliance and risk process and not only the cost of money but your cost of doing business and shareholder returns. At your stage in the game you know the boxes to check to reorganize. However, I want to point your attention to two areas that are often overlooked or undervalued: (1) asking compelling questions and (2) creating a pause in the action.

Asking a compelling question underlies the format of this book; as you have considered the questions, I trust that you have gained new insights and broadened your perspective and, as a result, sharpened your ability to act. Asking questions is a skill that all leaders have, but it often gets pushed aside by the temptation to provide answers. No one has all the answers. Asking a provocative question inspires people to think, to find new solutions and to blaze new trails. To succeed, step back from your day-to-day, reflect and list the questions that, if they are addressed (no: *when* they are addressed), will open onto new terrain—products, processes, and clients—for your organization. Consider: What will be the benefit, or what will be possible, as my organization (department, group, company) moves to the next level?

What if you ask a simple question?

"Do you realize that you are spending more on health care than on steel?" Dr. Deming asked during his 1982 visits to Pontiac Motor Division. No one had collected the data that Dr. Deming pointed to and no one had asked the question before at a General Management meeting. It wasn't until 2008 that the CEO of GM realized that health care added $1400.00 to each car and yes, GM was paying more for health care than it was for steel.

It is interesting to note that Pontiac and Ford Motor Company discovered Dr. Deming after a NBC Special posed the question "If Japan can, why can't we?" Quality and process improvements begin when you ask the right questions. Dr. Atul Gawande posed the "right questions" in the form of a "checklist" that he successfully applied, first in the operating room and now to two critically important transitions: the birth of a child and end-of-life care for the elderly. By asking simple questions, Dr. Deming and those who follow in his footsteps not only take their organizations to the next level, they also open new conversations for exploration. As you read further, keep top of mind the idea of asking questions to initiate organizational change.

Is it OK to begin with mission and vision?

Mission and vision are only the starting point. You know that it takes more than a vision and solid metrics to move your organization to the next level. As a leader you go beyond the adage "What gets measured gets done." You have attained your current role because you have demonstrated an array of skills and behaviors that inspire and mobilize your deep network of colleagues, clients and advocates. One reason for your success so far is that you are rightly seen as more than a "good communicator"; you generate conversations for action, and you have a keen ear for distinguishing a conversation for action from empty watercooler chatter. You have honed your ability to ask questions that ignite action and produce results. Your deep and strong relationships give you insight into your organization as a network of conversations and you understand that compelling conversations fuel action. You will move quickly beyond mission and vision to ask the questions, "What will it look like?" and "How will we get there?"

How can you begin?

So when you are offered the opportunity or the challenge to take your group, department or organization to the next level, begin with what others may view as the conventional approach: convene a meeting to align the mission, vision and goals with the new metrics or desired future state. *But,* do *not* launch into the mission/vision process in the rote fashion that is so familiar to all involved. Instead, with the understanding that the core engine that propels a new mission or vision is the language that defines it, introduce and own that language. Start a conversation to ignite change. Begin by posing a compelling question.

Here's an example from my own career. My first opportunity to initiate a conversation for action occurred when Governor William Weld appointed me Assistant Secretary for Public Safety for the Commonwealth of Massachusetts. The Legislature had recently passed a law called the 209A Restraining Order. The new law meant that a woman (or in rare instances, a man) no longer needed a witness to corroborate the assertion that her husband was beating her. This seems like an antiquated view today, but in 1991 the burden of proof rested on the victim.

My responsibility was to oversee the training of the state police and probation office on the requirements of the new law. To me, domestic violence was more than a law enforcement issue and I asked a question that sparked a conversation among a broad base of stakeholders: *How can we help women transition from lives of violence and lead violence-free lives for themselves and their children?*

Note: I didn't know the answer to the question. I didn't even know if anyone would be interested beyond my natural and immediate ally, Jane Doe, Inc./Massachusetts Coalition of Battered Women Service Groups. To my surprise, the question ignited a conversation that spilled beyond state law enforcement to include public health, business, Boston medical schools, the court system, probation and local law enforcement. In an unexpectedly positive response, stakeholders representing a wide diversity of views came forward. They offered their perspectives and suggested possible solutions, all inspired by the question.

The broad involvement led to new approaches; we were able to address areas where women fell through the cracks between law enforcement and the courts, the hospitals, housing and in the workplace. I was proud of recommendations made by the doctor who may have treated the same woman four times in seven months for injuries caused by "falling down the steps." The doctor's idea: to post discreet signs in every physician's changing room: "Are you a victim of domestic violence?" I was just as proud of the courageous decision of representatives of the District Court and Probate and Family Court who recommended being "on call" from Friday to Monday morning to issue temporary restraining orders so women (and some battered men) would not have to face the weekend in fear and in danger.

The point is, as a leader I posed a question that generated a conversation, inspired participation, ignited action and caused change. A new community was created: the constituents were formally organized into the Commonwealth's first domestic violence working group, which later became the Governor's Task Force on Domestic Violence, a model that other states would eventually follow. The Task Force evolved into the Governor's Commission on Domestic Violence, chaired by Lieutenant Governor Paul Cellucci after I was promoted to Secretary of Consumer Affairs and Business Regulation for the Commonwealth. The Commission has expanded its mission and remains active today. It is among my proudest accomplishments.

What is the best way to ask a question?

The question I asked the group began with the powerful word, "How?" When you are ready to take your organization to the next level, begin by asking two kinds of questions. "What" questions help to clarify the vision and mission; "how" questions elicit processes, actions, and/or solutions. Note the difference between: "What is next?" and "How can we reach the next step?" Know which questions to ask to move the process along to the next step in its growth.

The same basic rule applies to asking these questions as any other productive question: avoid yes/no or closed-ended questions. Ask questions that open new ground. Here are three ideas:

- Ask a compelling question or set an ambitious goal. For example, Steve Jobs challenged his team to design something truly revolutionary—light years ahead of any other product.
- Ask the "elephant in the room" question. For example, "How can we improve cycle time without adding cost?" Or, "How can we improve communications with our London office without stepping on corporate toes?"
- Ask a question that expands or provokes people to think differently. For me, it was "How do we help women transition from lives of violence?" that changed how people thought and created opportunity for innovative solutions.

Above all, always act with integrity: do not ask a question if you already know the answer or ignite a conversation in an area you are not going to fix.

If it makes you uncomfortable to put your people on the spot by asking a question that you don't have the answer to either, then don't do it. Remember that staying there depends on authenticity and integrity. In lieu of asking a question, you may choose to direct action with a powerful mandate in the style of President Kennedy, who in 1961 set the goal of landing a man on the moon and returning him safely to the earth by the end of the decade—a feat accomplished by Neil Armstrong on July 20, 1969. Whether you ask a question or set a goal, the desired result is the same: you want to ignite a conversation that compels and inspires.

How do you initiate the conversation to go to the next level?

Take Northeastern University as a case in point. During the tenure of three board chairs and two presidents, Northeastern University has transformed itself from a cooperative education commuter school with a reputation for engineering to a residential liberal arts school that values experiential education. As an alumna and a member of the Corporation, I remember when Northeastern broke with the past by selecting an "outsider" as president. With board support, Richard Freeland was selected to take Northeastern to the next level. I remember the meeting in which he announced the ambitious goal for his tenure: to make the *U.S. News and World Report* list of the top 100 colleges. It was not only an ambitious goal but a mobilizing conversation as well, because everyone—student, faculty, staff and board—was familiar with the rankings and President Freeland focused our attention on the criteria. The goal became a rallying cry and, in 2005, Freeland was at the helm when Northeastern earned a coveted place on the *U.S. News* list. Freeland had led dramatic institutional change and campus expansion. What could be next for Northeastern?

What's the next question?

In 2006, the board chose Joseph Aoun as its seventh president, with the charge to take Northeastern to the *next* level. The quest to move up in rankings on the *U.S. News* list continued, until the *Wall Street Journal* took notice:

In the past six years, Northeastern University has vaulted 42 spots in the powerful U.S. News & World Report college rankings. And not merely because it added programs, hired superstar faculty or built fancy facilities. The private school in Boston also has made an all-out effort to increase the number of applicants for admission, dispatching its 30-person recruiting staff across the country and sending hundreds of thousands of personalized letters and emails to high-school students. It persuaded more than 44,000 students to apply for one of the 2,800 spots in its fall 2012 freshman class.... Northeastern began broadening its outreach nearly a decade ago....

President Aoun didn't just continue the conversation; he deepened it by pointing the way for the university to have the "superstar faculty" and facilities that would create an exceptional reputation and brand.

A similar academic transformation was underway at Massachusetts Institute of Technology, Joseph Aoun's alma mater, where Susan Hockfield, the sixteenth president and first woman to hold the role, accepted the challenge to take MIT to the next level. MIT graduates are recognized for their technical acumen; however, many lack the social skills and facility to succeed in a globally interconnected role. It's OK to be a geek these days, but being a narrow and isolated geek is no longer acceptable. Not only did the curriculum expand to include more liberal arts classes, the criteria for acceptance broadened and, under President Hockfield, women grew to compose 52 percent of the student body.

How can you actively guide and manage the conversation?

You can expect the language and the conversations to change or evolve as your organization moves to the next level, whether from local to global, from domestic to emerging markets, from quality management to Six Sigma or from employee surveys to voice of the employee. The questions Joseph Aoun used to challenge the Northeastern community were different from the ones Richard Freeland posed. As the conversation evolves, your role is to guide it, and the way to steer a conversation is to ask questions. If customer focus and responsiveness are key to taking your organization to the next level, you will consistently seed your speeches, town hall meetings and 1:1 meetings with customer success stories and questions about accomplishments. You always ask, "How are we doing? What does the next step look like?" You will establish a topic of conversation and own the vocabulary. For example, it seems that all of my financial service clients talk about customer service, my academic leaders talk about the student experience and institutional advancement, while my defense clients talk about delivering technologies to the war fighter. They own the language.

Your goal is to get everyone on the same page. If everyone in your organization is speaking the same language it will be evident that you are on the "right" path. An important caution: conversations can disappear. That is why I urge managers and leaders to repeat the message over and over. It takes many repetitions before a conversation sticks. The words that you choose and the topics that are priorities cascade through the organization and infuse employee conversations and sometimes become fodder for positive office gossip. You might hear something interesting around the water cooler!

Sometimes leaders spend a lot of time getting buy-in, and in some cases they have to delay action when key people balk at the proposed changes. However, if you are able to get people to say the right words with integrity and consistency, you might find that their actions begin to align with their language. Simply put, it is very difficult for a person to say "Customers come first" and behave in the opposite way without tarnishing his personal brand, credibility and even integrity.

What are the consequences of not asking the right question?

If you have followed the succession of leaders at Hewlett-Packard, then you have probably noticed the inconsistencies, not only in their results but also in the various conversations that have been started, only to fizzle. Look at Carly Fiorna's experience. CEO Carly Fiorna was selected with fanfare to take HP to the next level. In the midst of the technology bubble, she sought to expand the company by diversifying into services—acquiring Price Waterhouse—and by growing—acquiring Compaq Computers. I am not commenting on the soundness of her strategy or its execution; I am calling your attention to the conversations that Carly tried to introduce, which did not take root.

Why? The business of HP was overshadowed by the conversations that surrounded Fiorna. They were all *about her*—the first female CEO of HP, "the most powerful woman in business." And being the center of conversation quickly became a negative for a previously private company. Not only was she in the spotlight, she was often "put on the spot," diverting attention from the message that she was trying to instill in her senior staff, her board and Wall Street. What began as a positive start—the first woman—devolved into a negative. The conversation almost always veered to her appearance and concerns about her being in over her head. In other words, Carly Fiorna was unable to introduce a compelling conversation and she was never able to take control of her brand and image at HP. Even the advertising campaign she launched, which featured Hewlett and Packard starting out in a Palo Alto garage, was viewed as an attempt at resurrection versus revitalization. It prompted the concerned chatter, "We are going backward, not forward."

I have ignited a conversation, now what?

My friend Maddy often cautions: Don't let an organization move faster than its ability to learn. In other words, give people time to understand, respond, ask questions, get comfortable with and then integrate the change. Few organizations have the courage to take the time to do things correctly. However, the benefits of going slow to go fast can ensure that an organization not only gets to the next level but *stays there*.

Press the Pause button. Now that you have created a conversational space, provide time for your colleagues or employees or your department or organization to integrate the new information, or just clear their heads before they take the next step. Why? Although we say that we can work at break-neck speeds with out pausing, we can't (see Chapter 7). I recommend that my coaching clients block out 30 minutes each day to review meeting notes, plan for their next meeting, or use the unscheduled time to *think*. To stay there you have to change your relationship to how you spend your time. At this stage of your career you realize that time—not money—is a precious commodity and that the way you use your time signals your organizational status and contributes to your staying power.

Pressing the Pause button is a tool that comes under the category of going slow to go fast. If you are running to back-to-back meetings, when do you get a chance to collect your thoughts and transition to the next meeting? As the leader of a group, department, function or organization you have the power to give people permission to pause. You can make it OK to take time to think and plan and reprioritize when necessary during the workday. For example, with the support of the CEO, we piloted a monthly program at Vertex. I described Third Wednesday as the ANTI-meeting. Third Wednesday has no agenda, no goal, and no expectations—indeed, that is its whole point.

What it is: 10:00 p.m. to 2:00 p.m. on the third Wednesday of the month, the Vertex community will press the Pause button to renew, reflect and think.

Introspective Vertexians will use this time to re-charge their batteries working solo or with one other person. We might see them reading, organizing their office or just staring out the window. By contrast, extroverts may use this time to lunch with a person they have been too busy to see, brainstorm a thorny idea or meet new people from other areas. Or you can go for a walk or join the meditation class.

There are only three ground rules: 1) The time is NOT to be devoted to completing current Vertex projects; 2) Ongoing work assignments or tasks are not to be communicated to others during this period; and; 3) The time is to be used in some mentally or physically active manner (catching up on sleep, for instance, would not qualify.) That being said, Third Wednesday will work on an honor system.

For extroverts (and introverts) who prefer structure, pre-organized events will be available, and might include film, book, music or theater discussions; exercises and games designed to reinforce group dynamics; meditation, yoga classes and other activities intended to stimulate new ways of thinking, enlarge perspectives or reinforce a sense of self. In short, anything that demonstates a pause from the day-to-day and that says, "I am re-energizing, reflecting, inventing and thinking."

Third Wednesday generates no documents, no products... unless by "product" you mean a creatively refreshed mind.

What it offers: Third Wednesday is intended as an antidote to rushing from activity to activity. Third Wednesday will encourage creativity free from predetermined objectives. It will thus increase the possibilities of serendipity—that wonderful moment in science or the arts in which that which is discovered is not that which was being sought.

Third Wednesday was successfully piloted but didn't stick and for good reason. The timing was not right. Vertex had to move at breakneck speed to introduce not one but two drugs into the marketplace.

Why does "walk the talk"
continue to have value?

Ann Mulcahy of Xerox maintained her connection to her colleagues whom she greeted by name. Mike Ullman of JCPenny blocked out time on his calendar to attend 26 two-day workshops reaching 700 associates, thirty attendees at a time. When asked how and why he found the time, he replied:

> I spent two days in a windowless room because I get to know my associates really, really well. They get to know their role in the company, I get to know them and they me. Frankly, [as CEO] I don't know what is more important than having people engaged.

There are many more examples of taking the time to engage employees, associates, peers and clients. They are authentic; "walking by" is not a drive-by in which employees are afraid to speak for fear of making a fatal impression. An open door is not a trap door where your frank comments convey you down a chute or ladder. On the contrary, when you have a conversation with an executive who has staying power, you leave the meeting feeling that the person has spent quality time with you. Executives with staying power are mindful, they are present, they listen and time seems to move more slowly when you are engaged in the conversation—"I can't believe it was only 15 minutes."

If you are not ready to designate a "Third Wednesday" or add meditation or yoga classes, perhaps you can end the practice of scheduling back-to-back on-the-hour meetings by reducing meeting times to 45 minutes. Or better still, have 10-minute stand-up meetings. Or you can follow the practice underway at audio company Sounds True, where they begin each meeting with "a good minute" of silence to create a break allowing people to start the meeting fresh.

What are the steps to successfully
move my organization to next level?

After you formulate and ask the question and create a space for people to pause and reflect, then what? Powerful processes can be set in motion, and it will be your job to direct them. Let the people who work for you bring all their intelligence and passion to bear on answering the question.

1 Introduce a compelling conversation or goal.

2 "Give the conversation away"—allow others to make the conversation their conversation.

3 Ensure that you have the support of your board/key stakeholders and that everyone speaks the same language.

4 Be visible and engaged.

5 Be authentic and, when necessary, fiercely guard the conversation.

6 Keep the conversation going by telling stories and celebrating successes.

7 Be courageous.

8 Breathe.

Now it's your turn. What new insights do you have and what actions will you perform to take your organization to the next level? Consider the following questions:

Question	Current	Future
What does taking my organization to the next level mean?		
Who are my supporters? Allies?		
Who will benefit? How?		
What is the "elephant in the room" issue that can become a rallying cry?		N/A
What's the iterative or breakthrough change I can lead?		
What would be a challenge or ambitious goal?		
What existing conversations can I leverage?		

Question	Current	Future
How can I create a break [pause] in the action?		
What can I do to ensure that meetings begin and end on time and that participants are emotionally present?		

17

Is It Time to Move?

Life moves on and so should we
— Spencer Johnson, *Who Moved My Cheese?* —

There comes a time to leave every role behind—whether you are moving up, out, or on. You don't have to be at the end of your career, and you certainly don't want to be at the end of your rope and forced to leave before you consider: Is it time to move? Follow Mike Ullman's advice: "If you are not learning, there is probably no reason to stay there." And if you are not learning, your departure will come as no surprise to your boss, peers and employees. Being alert and having the right timing put you in the right place at the right time; the key to "staying there" is moving by *your* choice. Move up, move out or move on—at the time of your choosing. So, that raises the question: What does it mean to stay?

Staying means that you have reached the significant position or vital role that you hoped and worked to achieve—for now. You landed in this role on plan or, to your surprise, ahead of schedule. When you consider your career progression, you may view your current position in one of four ways:

1 This is *the* position that will round out your brand and position you for your next role or
2 This position provides the visibility, credibility and networking opportunity to leverage to a new area of interest, a new company or a new venture; or
3 This position will be the capstone of your career and solidify your legacy; or
4 This? This really isn't work.

If you wouldn't describe your current position in one of these ways, it's time to shift from "staying there" mode to "getting there" mode again.

Is it time for you to move on?

If you are wondering, "Should I move?" the answer is likely to be *yes*. For one reason or another, the position has ceased to be a good fit; you have outgrown it, or you haven't produce the desired results, or your interests and energies are taking you in a new direction.

This isn't your first career move and it is unlikely to be your last. Along the way to your current position you have made a series of formative, well-timed choices. You know the importance of making the right move at the right moment. No matter why you are thinking about moving, it is critical to move while your stock is as high as possible (and if you sense your stock is sinking, bolster it before you go!). Your previous moves have been successful and well timed because you have been mindful of the signs—the appearance of your "it's time to move" patterns. For example, you find yourself thinking:

- "I am bored,"
- "I have done everything here that I can,"
- "This isn't what I thought it would be (my values and principles don't align)"
- "I am not making the contribution that I had hoped to make," or
- "I want to do something big."

You stay alert and attuned to your external and internal environments, and when you notice thoughts like these, you begin to consider the choices available or create new ones.

How do you feel about your current position?

The first step to answering the *Is it time to go?* question is to honestly examine how you feel about what you are doing now. Circle the word that best discribes your feelings for your current position:

Bored / Routine / Challenged
OK for now / Inspired / Passionate / Flow

If you have been in the role more than a year, consider anything below "inspired" as a "time to move" sign. If you are new to the role and feeling "challenged" in a negative way it is good to remember that you chose this opportunity as a stretch. Make certain that you and your manager are confident that you will surmount the challenges. If you have met and exceeded all the challenges this role offers, consider your next step. Two years ago, Lori had been inspired and passionate as she built up an innovative new department, but now she wondered:

> Is it time to leave? The work is starting to feel repetitive. I founded a new department and as a result we are reaching a population that was previously underserved. But that creative phase is over and now we are in maintenance mode—anyone could do it. I am proud to say that the Chamber recognized my work, especially the impact that the program has had and the fact that my approach was innovative. It was great to be honored for doing something that I really love. At the end of the event, I was surrounded by well-wishers and supporters. I wonder, is it time to find a larger playing field while my achievements are fresh in everyone's mind?

Yes, Lori is at the top of her game and the award by the Chamber signals that she passed the vetting process by an influential group of people. Her next step is to follow through with the specific aim of infusing her network with energetic ideas and new possibilities. She should start having discussions, inviting her network to envision her next role and help expand her choices. Her network of supporters will see opportunities for Lori to land in a bigger playing field and they will remind her that it is her choice to determine when (and how) she will move on.

Will you know when it's time to move?

Sharpen your observations. Pause, reflect and breathe. You begin with an awareness that *staying* does not mean forever. Just as you are never the last to leave a dinner or close down a bar—it just isn't who you are—you are organizationally savvy enough to know when the party is in full swing and when it is winding down. You are alert and attentive, aligned with all your key stakeholders and your organizational goals. If you are self-aware, mindful and intuitive, then you not only know how much time *you* have allotted to accomplishing the task at hand, but you can also accurately calibrate how your organization values you and your accomplishments. You have staying power because you are able to assess when your stock is on the rise and when it is on the decline or about to tank. You have learned by now that everyone has a "shelf life" and an expiration date.

Examine yourself through the eyes of your stakeholders and your managers or board. The questions are always the same: are you meeting or exceeding expectations? And, are you accomplishing your goals and, for some, securing your legacy? My friend Hensley often gauges progress by asking: Are you moving the needle?

Calibrate: How are you perceived regarding the expectations—yours and your stakeholders'—and what you have accomplished? How much time has elapsed? For example, if you've been in the role for less than six months and you are not meeting commitments and expectations, then you are in the wrong place. Exit before they ask you to empty your desk. On the other hand, if six months have passed and you are meeting expectations and achieving your goals and commitments with passion, use your network, your charm and your organizational savvy to ensure that this role is either a springboard to your next role or your crowning achievement. Remember, it is your choice.

What if you think you are going to be fired?

However, if your awareness, intuition and organizational savvy can be summed up as "bad vibrations," it is time to move on while you can do so on your own terms. Remember that it is easier to find a new job *if* you have a job, so don't quit in an emotional huff. You will have a tough time getting over it and, believe me, your organization will too. Don't tarnish your brand on your way out the door; instead, strive to make a lasting positive impression. Here are a few exit strategies:

- Zero in on an area or project where you can have a major visible win, exceed expectations and exit.
- Communicate with all major stakeholders, define or declare work to date complete and submit your resignation.
- Exit gracefully and without fanfare.

Four months into her new role as Director of Consumer Marketing, Paula was in trouble.

> I was so excited when I finally got this job—I had some great ideas for the new product line. But Ivan, my former boss and mentor, left the firm in a big shake-up and I hadn't developed the rapport with his rival that I should have. Lesson learned. Suddenly I'm not invited to important meetings. Human Resources hasn't approved two new hires, even though they were budgeted. A big campaign is floundering, in part because

my staff sees the writing on the wall. There's no way I can succeed in these circumstances. Better to manage a graceful exit, salvage as much of a win as I can, and move on.

Now is not the time to second-guess or hope. That will only let the clock run down. Remember to make moving on *your* choice. You recognize that you are not meeting the expectations and then decide to make your move. Self-aware, you accept accountability: you did not accomplish and contribute in the manner that you anticipated. Of course you will also want to ask *why*: Maybe you didn't ask enough questions? Or have deep enough relationships in the organization? Maybe the market shifted or priorities changed, or maybe there is new leadership and you no longer have access, power and influence. Yes, reflect and learn, but don't waste time going through everything you did (or didn't do) with a fine tooth comb, and don't trivialize by summing it up with "it was political." Instead start making or creating choices.

Now is a good time to lighten your load by finding humor in your situation. If you enjoy offbeat humor, I recommend singing the song "Always Look on the Bright Side of Life" from Monty Python's *Spamalot*. If you can't find a bright side, distract yourself by imagining all the ways your life or situation could be worse. Laugh now—really? Yes! Laughing increases the endorphins that are released in your brain while bringing in more oxygen to reduce stress. Try it!

> Yesterday is not ours to recover,
> but tomorrow is ours to win or lose.
> *Lyndon B. Johnson*

Move on. Make the courageous choice and activate your contingency plan: use your network and good will to let your advocates know that it didn't work out as planned and that you are actively looking.

What if you can't afford to move?

In Chapter 7 we talked about the importance of not separating your career from your life. However, if you truly believe that you *can't* move now, then you must go back to basics: clarify expectations; ensure that you have the right mix of skills on your team; meet 1:1 with all of your stakeholders with the intent of appreciating their perspectives, understanding their pain points and being engaging so that they seek you out for future conversations. Communicate, communicate and adjust your thinking to the new reality.

At the same time, find the low-hanging fruit and deliver results. It is imperative that you continue to do your best work. Treat your team with respect and dignity. Develop and encourage others and remember: No whining and no regrets. These are the basics—maybe one reason you find yourself in this situation is that you lost focus or minimized the importance of one of them. Now is the time to make the right choice: To double down and do your best work without being distracted by your plans to move on. This is a different kind of "staying there," and you must manage it very carefully in order to orchestrate a positive exit eventually. Under no circumstances can you allow yourself to be perceived as "marking time."

Establish a productive relationship with your boss and/or board. If they see you as borderline, focus on the deliverables. Schmoozing is likely to be misinterpreted—you won't be "one of the guys" until you clear the first hurdles. At the same time that you are preparing to leave on a high note, pause and reflect by addressing the following questions:

- Based on this experience, what have I learned?
- What do I want next?
- Where will my contribution be valued?
- What do I want to accomplish in this next opportunity?
- What is best for me (and my family)?
- Will I be challenged? Fulfilled? Inspired? Happy?

What if you want a new start?

Trish Karter made headlines when her all-natural and artisan product won the 1998 SOFI Award for its signature (and my favorite) Molasses Clove Cookies. But it wasn't just the cookies. Her recipe for Dancing Deer Baking Company's success as a national brand and industry innovator included an inner city location and a package of mission commitments that formed a "double bottom line" for the growing venture. In addition to making progressive commitments to the community and helping her employees move up the economic ladder, the firm donates 35 percent of the revenue from its Sweet Home product line to scholarships for homeless mothers, making a difference in the lives of children and families. In June 2010, after fifteen years at the helm of Dancing Deer, Trish made headlines when she announced, "In my next chapter, I'd like to have a bigger impact working with a product or concept that's more in the field of sustainability and social justice. I'm a builder and I think I've got one more big build in me." She refined that to put

C-Suite Mindset

STAY INVOLVED

Advisor: Jim Padilla
former President and COO, Ford Motor Company

There is a huge value to getting experience on an outside board. When you go on your first board, you will gain a much broader perspective not limited to just operational areas but envisioning where the company is going to be down the road. You also see how other organizations operate. It is critically important. Stay involved, seek out situations where you can add value and have fun.

guardrails around whatever she did next to include a positive impact on nutrition and dematerialization. This focused search eventually led her to developing new business models in urban agriculture.

You might say Trish earned the privilege of moving on to her legacy role, but she would say she stepped out on a ledge to allow her value system to lead her forward to new opportunities and risks with greater psychic rewards. She turned to her network of organizations and individuals with whom she has collaborated and shared inspiration over the years, finding her tribe to support her new ventures and aspirations.

How do you make the connection?

Your legacy chapter is where you support your passions full time. In Trish's case it's advancing the development of a whole new sector of urban farmers bringing production of healthier produce with a smaller environmental footprint to urban locations in the Northeast. Her "next chapter," LightEffect Farms, is the tangible expression of her passion for making a positive impact and her focused commitment to specific objectives. She feels strongly that she wouldn't have identified this market opportunity if she hadn't been very clear on her guardrails and kept looking until she found alignment.

The spark for your legacy project is likely to come from your community or philanthropic participation. In addition to his corporate boards, staying involved for Jim Padilla means serving as a mentor, as

C-Suite Mindset

BROAD PERSPECTIVE EQUALS BETTER PERFORMANCE

Advisor: Shelley Stewart Jr.
Chief Procurement Officer and Chair of the Board,
Howard Business School

You have to decide what you want to be good at. I decided that I wanted to be the best procurement person in the world and that's how I build my career and my brand. You can't be singularly focused—that is, only involved in your own industry. I am a better performer if I have outside involvement. I am the guy with all kinds of contacts. I deliver consistent performance and work never gets overwhelming: to stay on top you have to be on your game. I go on boards where I can make a difference and to do something different. I have a natural curiosity about things. I have curiosity and passion for what I do. Everything isn't about work all the time. I don't come home and think about work all weekend. I have balance in my life. When people ask me how I find time to do all the things that I do, I say—I make time and never at the sacrifice of my family. I enjoy what I do. It's fun.

chair of the Corporate Board of Advisors of the National Council of La Raza, and on the Hispanic Chamber of Commerce. It is no surprise that Jim Padilla received the highest award that the government of Mexico grants to a person not living in Mexico—the Ohtli Award.

You deftly apply your time, talent and treasure to areas that align with your values and principles. For example, for more than fifteen years CEO Mike Ullman has been the chair of the board for Mercy Ships International, an organization and state-of-the-art hospital ship that provides hope and healing to the forgotten poor. Shelley Stewart, Jr., a chief procurement officer, believes that mentoring is a part of his DNA because his father always had a mentee in tow. Guiding young professionals' career advancement flows naturally for Shelley. He used his expertise to create the first MBA in procurement at Howard University and it's no surprise that he gives his time generously as chair of the board of Howard Business School and as president of his local Boys

& Girls Club. In a similar vein, because she is a tenacious advocate for educational excellence, Yvonne Jackson served as chair of the board of Spelman College from 2004 to 2011, contributing her business acumen and business network to her beloved alma mater. Always a cultural bridge builder, Carolyn Chin took an active role in the formation of the Chinese American Committee of 100. And as for me, being a member of the board for St. Jude Children's Research Hospital in Memphis provided a warm welcome into a network that believes that "no child shall die in the dawn of life."

My friends keep asking: when are you going to stop working?

Executives who stay there have a rounded life of full expression—social, charitable, intellectual—and they excel at and enjoy what they do. They are comfortable in their own skins, they contribute to others and they are not struggling to get to the finish line. Work isn't the result of effort; it *flows*. Most important, these people have crafted and are living the life they choose. As a result, they may be going into the office every day but they have already stopped working—period.

What is your capacity for moving?

Some people find that next opportunity within their current organization, moving on while "staying." Others find that moving up means moving out. My own career has been a series of no-regrets "moves." Each opportunity I chose to accept was exciting and challenging and allowed me to use my creativity and innovate. I always viewed my career as a combination, an integration, of business, government and academics; as a result, I have been able to move easily from one domain to another. I admit, my career path isn't for everyone and when I compare it to that of my best friends who remained solidly in one organization twenty, thirty and even forty years I have deep respect for the choice they made—especially the ones who reached the pinnacle of their career and earned pensions by staying put.

But moving versus not moving isn't the defining factor of a successful career path. What is most important is the opportunity to grow versus being static, to contribute versus being a doormat and to be engaged and enthusiastic about your profession, your peers and the product of your labors. Only you can judge whether you can grow while "staying put," or if you will best evolve toward your own goals by moving on. But no matter where you find your next opportunity, remember that staying is never forever—eventually your curiosity or imagination will spur you to move on, up, or out. You will find your path by staying involved.

This above all:
To thine own self be true.
William Shakespeare

Add your thoughts and ideas below:

	Questions	Actions
ALERT?	<ul><li>What's going on here?</li><li>What do I want?</li><li>What do they think about me?</li><li>Am I inspired?</li><li>Have I "made it"?</li></ul>	
ADJUST?	<ul><li>Exit?</li><li>Stay?</li><li>Look for a new opportunity?</li><li>Am I a success?</li></ul>	
ALIGN?	<ul><li>Do my stakeholders support me?</li><li>My network ...</li><li>My family...</li><li>My community...</li></ul>	
ACT?	<ul><li>What choice will I make?</li><li>What is the right timing?</li><li>Am I acting appropriately now?</li></ul>	

Are You Asking Questions?

Judge a man by his questions
rather than his answers.

— Voltaire —

Now you have come full circle. I hope that, as promised, you have experienced that this book is about asking questions that are common sense but not commonly practiced. If you have taken a serious approach to the material you now have the tools to accelerate your ability to respond and adapt to change. In other words you are more agile. You are also more adept: You don't skip the tough questions or ignore the awful truth, you are guided by the answers and ready to explore new terrain. It all begins with a question. One question leads to another and up the spiral stairs you go with the credibility you earned and confidence you exude.

You now have a method, a practice, maybe even a checklist of questions that you pose whenever you encounter a new situation. When you walk into a room, chair a meeting, call your team together, a series of questions appear like a "dashboard" before you speak: Expectations clear? Actions aligned? Stakeholders on board? Network in place? Processes in place? If the answer to all is *yes*, you proceed. If it is *no*, you ask, "What am I missing?"

I hope that you have discovered that getting there means being clear about the questions that you need to ask to be successful. Each of us is unique; the hurdle that is likely to trip me up is not the same one you will confront. What you need to do to meet expectations and be clear on goals, roles and outcomes will be based on your environment and your unique communications preferences and styles. When you are getting there, the questions seem to come at you non-stop, from the macro to the micro: What value do I add? Do I have the right stuff? How can I anticipate change and not get stressed out? What if I fail? Will I get that next job? And in the process of getting there you are open to feedback—formal and informal. You seek out mentors, advocates and supporters and learn from them and you create a network of supporters who watch your back, all while performing exceptionally on the job. These guides alert you to changes underway and encourage you to decide in advance if you need (or want) to adjust your behavior to align with expectations or instead choose a different path. The good news is that in the process of getting there you have broadened your experiences and your horizon. You see yourself in a dynamic environment and you are engaged and productive. Aware of the opportunities, you naturally ask, "What's next?"

Staying there means staying involved

At this stage in your career you know that you don't have all the answers, and you stopped pretending that you did a while ago. Now you ask questions, listen to the answers and empower people to take the appropriate action. In the process, you find yourself with a group of followers who are alert to organizational changes and poised to offer ideas to close gaps in products, processes or service. They display agility. If you prefer, you can say they are "empowered." If the people around you—your followers—are empowered, you have staying power.

You now have the questions—the tools—to accelerate your career from being stalled, plateaued or landing in a ditch. As you navigate your career you have taken steps to stay relevant—you are curious, mindful and multidimensional. And staying relevant gives you the confidence to branch out and pursue new objectives. It is a full circle. Staying there means to keep something going, to continue leading or contributing at your level. In the process you are nurtured, nourished and inspired. As you lead your vibrancy will ignite others.

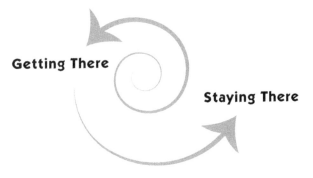

Getting There

Staying There

When you reach a place of success you remain aware, alert and thoughtful. You are seldom blindsided and rarely end up in the same mess twice. Why? You tailor the "getting there" questions to your new situation and you don't fall into the arrogance pit of "I made it." Bottom line: You respond to situations with agility. When you have to adjust or tweak your approach, style or perspective, you have the confidence based on experience to do so deftly. Stay on course. Ask yourself the tough questions now to eliminate the confidence and credibility sink-hole that always accompanies second-guessing and thoughts of should have, would have, and could have.

Ask peers, employees, stakeholders and clients questions, too. Given your role in the organization, people count on you to produce results and you are able to ignite conversations that inspire employees, peers and stake-holders to take action toward a new future. "People are our most important asset" is not an empty platitude. CEOs Josh Boger, Ann Mulcahy, Jim Padilla, Trish Carter and Mike Ullman are good examples—they walked the talk. How did they do it? They engaged their organizations by *asking questions:* Who is the best person for this job? How do we increase quality? How can we give back to our community? What can we do to enhance the customer experience? How can we reinvent our brand?

Staying involved is key to staying there. Your desire to learn new things, give back or meet new people leads you beyond your organizational walls and into your community, professional organizations, charitable giving or maybe learning a new instrument or taking on a new physical challenge. It's up to you and probably begins with the question *What is missing?*

What is next?

Remember, you have choice if you create it. Sometimes a little luck can make the difference, especially if you define luck as I do: *opportunity meets preparation.* Being agile will mean that the luck is mutual—you get the opportunity and they get an agile executive.

The formula is the same: be aware and know what *you* want; aim for clarity. Make adjustments but never either adjust your principles of integrity or sacrifice your family and friends. Ensure that you are in an organization and working with people who share your values and make damn sure that this is the place that will allow you to solidify your brand, hone additional skills or realize your aspirations.

Isn't it great to be in the driver's seat, behind the wheel, enjoying the ride? You picked the model of car, you determined the destination and you are moving at a comfortable or fuel-efficient speed. And you are aware that you are scanning your environment and asking the appropriate questions: Is there a speed trap up ahead? Will the traffic ease up? You drive along effortlessly, alert, and continually making the appropriate adjustments. Effortlessly.

For example, Sydney has developed the skills to succeed in a very hierarchal organization because she couldn't pass up the opportunity to work on a project with global reach. Yes, they recruited her, but she *chose* them. After three years, she describes her situation:

> All the resources that I requested I now have: my program manager is amazing and so is my Deputy Director. We continue to sort out roles but there are no conflicts – we complement each other. Really, everything is in order as we move into the final phase of this project. The interest and visibility are exploding. There are a lot of demands on my time so I am really paying attention to time management. I now take things step by step and delegate, delegate, delegate. As for me, I wonder, is it time to transition?

Time to transition? What a great question! This book is built around questions. Throughout this book you have been asking yourself questions, working to find the answers that work for you at this time in your career. You can revisit these questions at another time and the answers might be different. The important thing is to keep asking the questions.

Priscilla Douglas is well known by top executives as a skilled adviser and coach. Priscilla coaches individuals en route to the C-suite and executives in the C-suite to be more skillful at working collaboratively and strategically. She helps advance leadership skills for major clients in financial services, biotech, government, higher education, architecture and defense.

Priscilla's ability to help others unlock higher leadership value can be attributed, quite simply, to the fact that Priscilla is a leader herself. Earning her doctorate from the Harvard Graduate School of Education in four years, elected class marshal, she was then selected by a Presidential Commission to serve as White House Fellow and as special assistant to the director of the FBI. Her public service for the Commonwealth of Massachusetts includes being assistant secretary for public safety, launching the Governor's Task Force on Domestic Violence, as well as initiating Hate Crimes Tracking. In addition, she successfully introduced the techniques of total quality management across the Commonwealth, which led to an invitation by the Australian Parliament to keynote the launch of their quality initiative.

Priscilla has held senior leadership roles in Fortune 200 companies and most recently at entrepreneurial Vertex Pharmaceuticals. She continues to grow and share her knowledge as a board member for Landmarks Orchestra, Innovation Institute at Massachusetts Tech Collaborative, Northeastern University, Cycling Through History, Boston Museum of Science and Leader Bank. Priscilla was an instructor in the masters program for Harvard University Radcliffe Seminars, and taught courses in management, leadership and organizational behavior. She is currently on the faculty of the International Women's Forum.

Priscilla is passionate about her work and her 1:1 client relationships. Her workshops are dynamic and her speeches are impactful. You can count on her to inspire by example and interact so each person she reaches achieves personal and professional satisfaction and success.

Getting There and Staying There

"Priscilla Douglas has written an outstanding book that will make all of us think about what it means to be a leader. The book is a wonderful example of the ways those with no experience or with lots of experience can approach being leaders in business.

This is must-read--a necessary read for anyone thinking about taking on challenges to meet 21st century opportunities for leaders in business. I recommend this book in the strongest possible terms."

—*Charles J. Ogletree, Jr.*
Jesse Climenko Professor of Law, Founder and Executive Director,
The Charles Hamilton Houston Institute for Race and Justice

"This book has an active approach to self reflection, self inquiry, and self coaching. The questions truly challenge you. *Getting There and Staying There* is unique because it provides clarity on the 'right' questions that will stimulate personal and professional growth. Engaging! Thought provoking! Insightful! I recommend this book to all my advisors, mentors, peers, mentees and to anyone who is looking for tools that will guide them to finding the right next step. This is a book that I will read again and again!"

—*Laurie Zephryin, MD*
Director of a national women's health program

"Priscilla Douglas has finally put to paper, in a delightful, easy-to-read and meaningful volume, the incredible advice she has shared with so many of us who've benefitted from her one-on-one coaching.... Her emphasis on self examination and reflection, adjusting my perspective and forcing me to think and see differently, and her direct, no-nonsense approach have been critical in my own professional maturation.... and the key to much of my success. How fortunate that so many more will benefit from Priscilla's brand of mindful self reflection.... and that as a consequence of her wonderful book folks like me can carry her reminders in our pockets. This is a must-read for all mid-level professionals working their way to the top."

—*Binta Brown*
2012 Fortune *Magazine "40 under 40" Business Leader*

"Priscilla Douglas has provided a most practical guide to mastering your corporate career. By leveraging her own exceptional corporate and government success, she has provided this must-have strategy of asking yourself the practical questions that should be considered based on the most important times and indicators of your career path. I strongly recommend this book to all corporate executives with a particular focus on those who are on the path to the C-Suite!"

—*Ronald L. Walker II*
Managing Partner and President, Next Street Financial, LLC

Made in the USA
Monee, IL
10 February 2021